L. Vernon Caine

To Heights Beyond

THE STORY OF ILLINOIS COLLEGE 1955–1973

L. VERNON CAINE

President Emeritus Illinois College

May thy years increase by hundreds,
Proud as those already gone.
May the lamps thy founders lighted
Lead thee e'er to heights beyond.
—*from the alma mater,
Ruth Badger Pixley '18*

Published for
Illinois College
by
Southern Illinois University Press
Carbondale and Edwardsville

Copyright © 1986 by The Trustees of Illinois College
All rights reserved
Printed in the United States of America
Edited by Susan H. Wilson
Designed by Quentin Fiore
Production supervised by Kathleen Giencke

Jacket illustration: Rammelkamp Chapel

Library of Congress Cataloging in Publication Data

Caine L. Vernon, 1904–
   To heights beyond.

   Includes index.
   1. Illinois College—History. 2 Universities and colleges—Illinois—Jacksonville—History.
I. Title.
LD2341.I52C34   1986   378.773'463   85–14237
ISBN 0-8093-1253-0

89 88 87 86   4 3 2 1

*To Elizabeth
who was a full partner in all of it*

CONTENTS

Illustrations ix
Foreword xi
William N. Clark
Preface xiii
Acknowledgments xv
Introduction xvii
Donald C. Mundinger
1. Genesis: 1955–1956   1
2. The New Administration Takes Shape: 1956–1960   18
3. The 1960s Begin: 1960–1962   58
4. Growth and Change: 1962–1964   83
5. Golden Years: 1964–1967   105
6. A Time of Bewilderment: 1967–1970   124
7. The End of an Era: 1970–1973   153
8. Conclusion   168
Appendix A. To Heights Beyond: The Inaugural Address, October 19, 1956   177
Appendix B. Who Runs the College?   186
Appendix C. Commencement Remarks to the Class of 1973   189
Index   193

ILLUSTRATIONS

L. Vernon Caine	frontspiece
Elizabeth Caine	v
President Caine and Dr. Fred Hoskins	21
The Caine family and Mrs. Charles Rammelkamp	22
Book and track medal belonging to William Jennings Bryan	37
Harry J. Dunbaugh '99	72
Dr. George Baxter '96	74
Rammelkamp family members at the dedication of Rammelkamp Chapel	81
Charles Percy	87
Three oldest alumni attending Alumni Luncheon, 1963	89
Governor Otto Kerner	97
Participants in the 1964 Harvard International Debate Tournament	99
The Caines	113
The Caine Student Center	131
Honorary degree recipients at 1967 Commencement	132
The trustees of Illinois College, 1968–1969	138
Reception for Ralph Smith '37	147
Shirley Friend and her portrait of President Caine	150
The Class of 1970	157
Secretary of Defense Melvin Laird	160
Trustees' presentation to the Caines	166
Naming of the Caine Student Center	169
Illinois College faculty, 1972–1973	172

FOREWORD
William N. Clark
Chairman of the Board of Trustees of Illinois College
1966–1981

The years between the mid-1950s and the mid-70s were perilous ones for higher education in the United States, the more so because some of the perils masqueraded as opportunities begging to be exploited. Beguiled by the prospect of an endlessly expanding market of young people in a climate of eternal prosperity, many colleges and universities undertook programs of building and borrowing that were to tax them sorely later on. For some institutions the problems caused by overexpansion proved fatal.

The lives of college administrators were further complicated during those years by manifestations of a spirit of rebellion and disdain for authority on the part of a sufficient number of students to seriously disrupt educational programs on many campuses.

Illinois College bears no scars from these and other problems that confronted educators in the period. Indeed, the college improved year by year in such critical areas as faculty quality, financial strength, and condition of the physical plant. At no time were its financial statements marred by red figures.

That these favorable conditions prevailed at Illinois College in such trying times was the consequence, first and foremost, of strong and courageous leadership provided by L. Vernon Caine, its president from 1956 through 1973. President Caine brought firmness, determination, and a disciplined approach to finance to the College when these

characteristics were much needed. That Illinois College prospers today under the able guidance of his successor testifies to Dr. Caine's dogged adherence to his own operating style.

At the same time, he and his lovely wife, Elizabeth, created an atmosphere of grace and warmth in the president's home that added immeasurably to the attractiveness of campus life during the Caine years. I commend his story to all who believe in the mission of the liberal arts college and cherish its contribution to our society.

PREFACE

This book is not strictly a history, although it recounts the events of an eighteen-year period in the life of Illinois College. Nor is it a memoir, for it leaves out most of the Caine family history. Instead, it is intended to give flavor and meaning to a vibrant era in the long history of an important institution.

It is my hope that this book will leave the readers with some understanding of the generosity and sacrifice of many people who were the builders of this time. I was fortunate to be the president and thus the coordinator of the efforts of many who made these great years a bright chapter.

While it is not possible to mention many of those whose contributions were significant, it is only fair to acknowledge the unique contribution of my wife, Elizabeth. She was not only a good wife and mother, she was a peerless helpmate and a talented First Lady for the College. She was loved and respected by everyone. Elizabeth did her best for Illinois College and for its faculty and students. In 1970, Elizabeth was stricken with cancer and, after a valiant battle, died in 1980. She left her mark on the campus and bettered and brightened the lives of many.

It should be remembered that not only those of our days but people spread over a century and a half—the students, faculty, trustees, alumni, and friends, and nine previous presidents—had roles in the drama of which my administration was only a recent part. Through good times and bad, through

Preface

depressions and wars, and through all the vicissitudes of public life since the Yale Band days, the College survived and is today stronger than ever before.

The reason it has come so far is summed up in the words of Bruce Catton, the great Pulitzer Prize-winning Civil War historian and former editor of *American Heritage,* on whom I had the honor of bestowing a doctor of laws degree when he was our 1958 Commencement speaker: "It is the noble dreams of men that live the longest.—The evil is short lived. It is the good that survives. It survives in bricks and stones, in human institutions that go on working long after the men who founded them have been gathered to their fathers. It survives in the hearts of men who—re-examine their debt to the past."

To those who worked with me in the ordering of Illinois College for those eighteen years, I conclude with words from the mystical poet Gibran, which I quoted at the dinner given by the faculty for Elizabeth and me as we concluded our era:

Farewell to you and the years I spent with you,
It was only yesterday that we met in a dream—
—now our dream is over.
If in the twilight of memory we should meet once more,
We shall speak to each other
And if our hands should meet in another dream
We shall build a tower to the sun.

L. Vernon Caine

ACKNOWLEDGMENTS

In addition to the people who were participants in the Caine administration, I am particularly indebted to those who had a part in getting this material ready for publication.

Judy Sandman, who does my secretarial work at the College, helped me in getting the material and the photographs together. June Pavlick typed the semifinal manuscript, and Virginia Green entered the final draft into the computer. She was able to use the fearsome machine for the first time owing to Professor Don Filson's assistance and supervision. His help was invaluable.

Robert Merris, from his extensive experience as a newspaperman, corrected errors of style and usage. Professor Ruth Bump proofread the final manuscript. She did the job properly—the result of both a lifetime spent teaching English and her experience as a professional proofreader. Professor Iver F. Yeager did much for the enterprise. He read the manuscript for factual errors and suggested revisions and corrections. His experience editing two other Illinois College publications was put to good use in the production of this volume.

President Donald C. Mundinger is responsible for the publication of this book. I am grateful to him for that, but I am more so for his leading the College to new heights as my successor.

INTRODUCTION
President Donald C. Mundinger

This book is a history of a period in the development of Illinois College and the personal recollections of Dr. L. Vernon Caine, president of Illinois College from 1956 through 1973.

The history is important for two reasons. First, it is a record of a dynamic period in the development of Illinois College. These pages are significant to those who love Illinois College, students of higher education, and historians. Illinois College conferred the first baccalaureate degree in Illinois in 1835. We acknowledge a special responsibility to maintain an accurate and complete history of the College work. This Caine volume is a companion to those covering earlier periods.

Second, this volume recalls the work of many who, because of their love for old Illinois College, worked heroically to build a College from the nadir of the post–Korean War years to the strong institution of the early 1970s, when Dr. Caine retired. Thus, these pages are a record and recognition of those who loved and sacrificed to nurture a vision of excellence and service.

As Dr. Caine's successor, I ask license to comment on his work at this College. I was told frequently in my early years at Illinois College—and continue to be told to this day—that Dr. Caine was a strong financial man and manager. To be sure, he was that. But, he had three strengths that proved far more important. Dr. Caine had an uncanny ability to pick

Introduction

good people, faculty, and students. Those people are some of the gifted members of today's faculty and comprise our loyal body of alumni. Dr. Caine also had, and has, a speculative sense of what is excellent and what will have future importance. Experimental, yet prudent; visionary, yet solid. And Dr. Caine understood and lived by a code of loyalty and work: loyalty to God, family, and College, and also hard work in their cause. His work for the College continues today as he visits with alumni and friends. As president emeritus, he has accepted the special challenge to build the endowment of the College through bequests and estate planning.

I am pleased to commend this book to you because it is enjoyable and thoughtful. It honors a special band of people who drove the stakes of the College deeply, making it possible for today's generation to strengthen and lengthen the cords—the cords of quality, service, and vision.

1
Genesis:
1955-1956

Among the letters that reached me one morning in early October 1955 was one destined to change our lives. It was from a man unknown to me—Dr. C. Ellsworth Black '16, chairman of the committee on a new president for Illinois College. He informed me that a mutual friend, Russell W. Kohr, Director of Public Information at Lake Forest College, who had been on the staff of Illinois College the year before, had suggested me for the presidency. He would like to have my credentials if I had any interest in being considered for the position.

We were living in St. Paul, Minnesota, where I had a secure and challenging position as vice president of Macalester College. We liked it there. Our oldest son, Clifford, a graduate of Macalester, was studying in the law school at the University of Minnesota. Alan was attending Macalester College, and Stanley was a sophomore at Central High School. We had moved there from Jamestown College, Jamestown, North Dakota, in 1950, where I had occupied a variety of teaching and administrative positions, ending up as vice president and acting president.

At the same time, we were also pondering two other offers that would have been radical changes from the life we had known for so long. One had been put to me through the Board of Ecumenical Missions of the Presbyterian Church. The church had just turned over most of its foreign missionary enterprises to native management. One such institution

was Silliman University in the Philippines. Things were not working out well, and the board had imposed certain constraints on native management if it was to continue to support the institution. A new Philippine president was to be named, and two Americans approved by the board were to be given rather broad managerial powers. They wanted me to be vice president and a member of the Board of Trustees. The soon-to-be announced Philippine president was the Islands' consul in Chicago. He came up to see me about taking the position. The main disadvantage was that it was an awkward time to go abroad as far as the family was concerned. Since the appointment would have been for at least four years, I decided that leaving the United States at that point in my career was not the wisest choice.

The second offer was to join one of the nation's foremost professional fund-raising firms with headquarters in New York City. It conducted financial campaigns for nonprofit organizations, such as colleges and hospitals, all over the nation. To my protestation that I did not want to live in New York, they said I could just as well live in a place of my choice in the Midwest. The chief inducement was an income some three times as much as I ever hoped to make in academic life. I had agreed to come to New York to talk about the position before I received Dr. Black's letter.

I did not know much about Illinois College, and I had never been to Jacksonville. I had met a few of its administrators and was well acquainted with Russell Kohr. In Presbyterian college circles, it was known that all was not well at Illinois College. There had been troubles with its church relationship to such a degree that there was talk of dropping it from the group. A rather extensive survey made of all the Presbyterian church related colleges had resulted in a confidential report of the strengths and weaknesses of each of the group. I had access to that report, which gave the College high marks academically but noted severe management prob-

Genesis

lems and a dangerous financial situation that rendered the future of the College uncertain.

Without any idea as to whether or not I would accept an offer of the presidency, I sent back the requested information. Before the end of the month, I had a call from Dr. Black asking that Elizabeth and I come to Jacksonville for an interview. I learned later that the trustees had used some on-the-scene investigators to delve into my suitability. There were two or three alumni in the Twin Cities, chief of whom was Ray Hartman '13, vice president of Munsingware. Because of my commitments, including that trip to New York, it was not possible for us to go to Jacksonville until Thanksgiving week.

We arrived in Springfield by train on a Monday night and had some difficulty finding Professor George Horton, who was to meet us. He surmised that anyone who was a candidate for the presidency would be in the chair car. Instead, we were traveling coach. He took us to the guest apartment in Baxter Hall where we met professors Eleanor Miller and Ethel Seybold, the other two members of the Selection Advisory Committee from the faculty. After some light refreshment, we were left to sleep for the first time on the campus of Illinois College.

Tuesday was a long and very busy day of interviews and inspection. That evening, a reception for us was held at the home of Robert Capps, vice chairman of the board, with all of the trustees and their wives from the Jacksonville area in attendance. We had a good time and were favorably impressed. After a busy Wednesday morning, we took the noon train from Springfield to Chicago. We went to the office of Frank Elliott '99, president of the Harris Bank, to be looked over. He took us in his chauffeured Cadillac to Oak Park to meet the board chairman, Dr. Fred Hoskins '26, pastor of the First Congregational Church.

We had a delightful dinner with Dr. and Mrs. Hoskins, and

we caught the night train home in time for our waiting family to go out to eat Thanksgiving dinner, as was our custom, with football coach and athletic director of Macalester, Dwight Stuesey, and his family. Dwight had been the quarterback for the University of Illinois the year one of the all-time greats of football blazed his way to immortality. Red Grange was a sophomore when Dwight was a senior.

Within surprisingly few days, a letter arrived from Dr. Black including what he called "suggested terms of employment" and inviting me to comment upon them. My reply was that the terms were satisfactory but, before I could accept, I would want to talk further with them about some conditions that had nothing to do with salary or living arrangements. I outlined my concerns in a rather lengthy letter and said I would have to come down and talk about them before I could make any decision.

In spite of my noncommittal reply, a special meeting of the board was called on December 16, 1955, to hear the report of the committee. They recommended my appointment, and the board unanimously adopted a resolution to that effect. It was transmitted to me by Dr. Garm Norbury '12, secretary.

Now the ball was in my court. I had been to New York for the interview there, had been offered the position, and had turned it down. Money was no substitute for the challenge and joys of college leadership—the way I wanted to spend the most productive years of my life. We also had decided against going to the Philippines. Now it was either go to Jacksonville or stay at Macalester.

During the Christmas recess, I came alone to Jacksonville to discuss some of the changes that I thought had to take place if the College was to recover from its serious difficulties. Only if these matters were agreed upon would I feel it proper for me to accept the presidency. I had given the matter the most thorough consideration and I was perfectly frank with the board. The members had read the letter outlining my thinking before I came to talk.

Genesis

In weighing the pros and cons of accepting the presidency, I found there was much on the plus side. The College was an old and highly respected institution with an illustrious record of service. It had a Phi Beta Kappa chapter, a rare distinction for a very small college. It had trained more distinguished people than any small college I had ever known. It had a strong faculty academically, and Jacksonville was an attractive place to live.

The negative aspects were formidable. The enrollment had sunk so low that without an increase of at least 50 percent in the very near future, the College was doomed. For six years the College had not been able to balance its operating budget, and the accumulated deficit was equal to about three quarters of its annual expenditures. Only the most essential repairs had been made for many years, and the buildings and equipment would require large expenditures to bring them back to acceptable standards. Some $182,000 in assets, including $125,000 of the Rockefeller gift for endowment, had been liquidated in order to supply necessary cash for operations.

At least as bad as the enrollment and finances was the problem of relationships. The College had been without a president for six months and the previous incumbent had served but two years marked by increasingly serious turmoil. Part of the problem had to do with MacMurray College, the nearest academic neighbor only a mile away.

MacMurray was an old and highly respected college for women. Women's colleges had fallen upon hard times, and many were becoming coeducational in order to survive. MacMurray had suffered precipitous declines in enrollment and was in a precarious financial situation as a result. Since both colleges in Jacksonville were in trouble, the solution to the problem for many seemed to be a union, or at least close cooperation. Mergers or cooperative arrangements of this sort were taking place elsewhere. The two colleges appointed committees to examine the options. Not being informed as to just what was going on, townspeople, alumni, students,

and faculty listened to all sorts of rumors. Some thought Illinois College was to become a men's college and MacMurray would enroll only women; others believed the two colleges were to become one. In any case, Illinois College people seemed to think that their institution was going to come out on the short end of whatever happened. President William K. Selden, a proponent of some sort of connection, became a casualty, serving only two painful years.

When Illinois College broke off negotiations between the two colleges and decided to be what it had been before, the excitement subsided but the animosities were longer lasting. The loss of good will and the divisions within the organization would be a serious handicap for a new president. Feelings about this and other problems were so strong within the College that half the faculty left over a period of two years and enrollment was reduced to a dangerous level.

Less obvious but of critical importance to the future of the College and to the prospects of success for a new president was a kind of anarchy that prevailed on the campus. Nobody seemed to be in charge. Various members of the board exercised certain administrative powers, and disgruntled members of the faculty had been going to individual board members rather than to the president to have their problems resolved.

A prime example of the disarray was the way the College was managed when President Selden departed. Not without some valid reasons, instead of naming an acting president from within the organization, a triumvirate was constituted as the head. It consisted of two board members and the dean of the College. The members of the board were Frank Rantz, president of the Elliott State Bank, Jacksonville, and Benjamin Thomas, the noted Lincoln scholar and author from Springfield. When it became necessary for someone to sign as the chief administrative officer, Dean Ernest G. Hildner, Jr., was designated as "Acting President for Academic Mat-

Genesis

ters and for Fund Raising in connection with the Associated Colleges of Illinois."

In spite of what looked like a "sea of trouble," it seemed to me that under the proper circumstances the difficulties could be corrected and the College launched on a new course. It would depend upon the willingness of the board to agree to certain changes. Only if agreement could be reached would I accept the presidency.

The necessary changes, as I saw them, were in philosophy and management rather than in the nature of the College or its external relationships. The College must reaffirm its Christian commitment and practice what it preached. Actually, the board had already made the decision and one of the reasons Dr. Hoskins, a clergyman, had been named chairman of the board a few months earlier was to demonstrate that reorientation. The more difficult matters were the restoration of administrative order and sound business practices. The board readily agreed to refrain individually and collectively from administration. It would set policies that were binding on the president and all others but the president would administer the policies. All faculty-related matters, except those covered by the bylaws, would be handled by the president. The trustees readily and unanimously agreed to these terms and were unwaveringly true to the agreement from then on.

On the very last day of 1955, I wrote a letter accepting the presidency of Illinois College and agreed to take over on February 1. Late in January, Elizabeth and I with our son Stanley and our oversized mongrel cat, who became a campus figure in his own right, moved into the gracious home. The other two boys helped with the move but they were never there for long. We lived there until June 30, 1973.

I had expected to have about a week to get settled before going to the office on the appointed date, but the day after our arrival I was told of an important meeting of the educa-

tional leaders in Springfield the following day. It was suggested that I attend. I went, and for nearly eighteen years there was always something that needed to be done. Although I became very tired at times, I never grew weary of the job to which I was committed. All my life seemed to have been preparation for what I was doing. While I had several chances for positions that may have constituted professional advancement, I never seriously considered the possibility of taking another position.

As long as I live I shall not forget the first morning's walk to the office. It was always a thrill to me to walk around the side of ancient Beecher Hall, the oldest college building in Illinois, down the brick walk amid the fine trees and flowering shrubs in season, past noble Sturtevant, and down the incline to Tanner. But it was an unusual sight that made me remember that first walk. I was not thinking of the fact that each of these buildings was named for an illustrious predecessor of mine, and it never entered my head that someday a building would be named for me also. I was thinking about what I should do first that day.

The sight that jarred me out of my reverie came abruptly. The door of Jones Chapel was flung open, and the entire student body came thundering out of the building as if the place were on fire. As the students raced toward Tanner, where I was headed, they strung out in a ragged procession with those most fleet of foot outdistancing their slower classmates. I soon found out that this extraordinary spectacle signaled neither a catastrophe nor an athletic event. It was the opening day of the semester, and the race was to get to the registration tables first.

All the students had assembled in the chapel to get instructions for registration, which was to take place in Tanner. Then it was every man for himself. The one who got there first registered first, while the others stood in line. How long you stood in line and whether or not you got your choice of classes and sections depended upon where you were in the

Genesis

line. When I found out what was going on, I decided that we would find a better way to register students for classes before the opening of the next semester.

Waiting at the office was Mrs. Wilmith Gillham, who had been secretary to my two predecessors. She was about my age and she retired when I did. I could not have gotten along without her; she remembered everything and was wise and efficient.

The historic desk at which I was to sit was piled high with things that had to be done. Many of them were overdue. In addition, nearly every member of the faculty and no small number of students had asked to see me as soon as possible. They all wanted to get a word in before I made any decisions. It seemed, too, that almost every organization in Jacksonville and many from the surrounding area wanted the new president to address them on a variety of topics. I took a deep breath and, with Mrs. Gillham's assistance, began to sort out what was to be done and in what order.

Not choice but circumstance dictated what had priority. The College catalogue was overdue at the printer's but was being held up to see whether or not the president thought tuition should be increased. The major project on hold was a new women's dormitory.

Several months before, the board had applied to the Housing and Home Finance Agency (HHFA) for a loan to construct a dormitory for women, the first Illinois College project specifically related to women. I had hardly settled in my chair (I had no previous knowledge of the project) when word came that tentative approval had been given for the financing. The College was given ninety days to select a site, employ an architect, and deliver preliminary plans for evaluation by the agency. At a hastily called meeting of the board's Executive Committee, I was instructed to contact and evaluate architects and to call a joint meeting of the Executive and Buildings and Grounds committees to sanction further actions. I had no knowledge of any architectural firm in Illinois.

Four firms were contacted, and my choice was Mittlebusher and Tourtelot of Chicago, who had designed the dormitory which had been built in 1954. This firm was approved, and by the time the ninety days were up (April 30) the requirements had been met. The proposal was accepted, and the loan was authorized by the end of July.

While I had been aware of the charades and red-tape entanglements of federally funded projects, I began to learn even more. The first requirement for getting the actual loan was to take bids from private institutions for the construction loan. Since the government was going to bid 2.75 percent, no one else would have the slightest interest in bidding. In spite of that it was necessary to advertise and await the prescribed time before turning to the government. With the money assured, the contract was put up for competitive bids, and Hugh Gibson began construction at the end of October. Ground was broken as a Parents' Day event. Construction progressed at a good pace, and the building was ready for occupancy the following fall.

One of the conditions of the loan was that the trustees should establish parietal rules for residents of the dormitory. The rules were calculated to keep conditions attractive to those who lived on the campus and to prevent undue wear and tear on the building. Pets and cooking in rooms were forbidden and quiet hours were established. These rules were to be in effect until 1996, when the contract would expire. I doubt that today anyone knows that these rules remain in force and that any violation makes the College immediately liable for payment of the balance of the loan. Such an event would be a tragedy because the College cannot afford to pay off a 2.75 percent interest loan when it can now invest its money for several times that figure.

In spite of all this expeditious action, I was troubled over the construction of this dormitory. I was not aware that it was authorized when I came to the College and, while it

Genesis

turned out to be a wise and timely project, it did not appear so when I first reviewed the situation. The application for construction funds was based on sheer optimism. There was more than enough room in Crampton Hall for all the women and Fayerweather House was empty. As for men's housing, the new dormitory was only partly full, and its income did not begin to pay for its operation and the amortization costs. The new dormitory for women would have been a disaster unless enrollment increased rapidly. It did, but how were we to know?

One of the problems the trustees had informed me would require immediate attention was the business operation. They could not have been more right. The Business Office was an operation from the previous century. Accounts were handwritten in ledgers and there was no way for keeping up to date. It was months after the end of the fiscal year before the results of the previous year's operation could be determined. A number of people authorized the expenditure of funds, and there was no uniform accounting of a number of special funds. When I had studied the situation, I outlined a radical modernization that went to the board. The chairman of the board and I were given the responsibility of installing a new system of business operations.

Although I had some business knowledge and had even served as acting business manager for a few months at another college, I wanted my suggestions to be reviewed by someone who was more of a specialist; Dr. Hoskins concurred. He suggested the business manager of the Chicago Theological Seminary, who came down for a few days to review our situation and our proposal.

It was obvious that we needed machine bookkeeping and a complete overhaul of business practices. We were fortunate to locate an almost new accounting machine, which was being disposed of by the University of Chicago Medical

School because it was changing over to a computer operation. It cost us only $3,000 and was still in use at the time of my retirement.

Most significant was the adoption of a new set of business guidelines. Over the objections of some faculty members, every dollar collected by any agent of the College had to be turned over to the Business Office for accounting. No purchases could be made without the permission of the business manager, who could allow expenditures only pursuant to budget authorization. If a proposed expenditure was not budgeted, authorization would have to be obtained from the Finance Committee before it could be made. Larger purchases could not be made except pursuant to bids. The new regulations and the new accounting system transformed the management of the College.

Not long after my arrival, the business manager resigned, and a man who was a complete stranger to the situation, Carroll R. Wilson, a businessman from Grove City, Pennsylvania, replaced him.

No discussion of the Business Office is complete without reference to Mrs. Leah Schramm, second in command there. Like Mrs. Gillham in the president's office, she had been with the College for years. She continued to serve beyond my administration. Self-effacing to a fault, she nevertheless was the anchor of the operation.

In 1955, the immensely wealthy Ford Foundation divested itself of some billions of dollars by announcing substantial grants to every private, four-year college in the nation. Payable in 1956, these grants were to function as endowment for ten years and then could be used in any way the institution saw fit. A formula had been devised whereby each institution could figure the size of its own grant, and it had been determined that Illinois College would receive $75,000. In going over the figures, I discovered an error and called it to the attention of the foundation. As a result, the College received $104,500.

Genesis

Another problem I was asked by the trustees to look into as soon as possible was the relationship with the Alumni Association. The Alumni Association of Illinois College is the fourth oldest in the nation, antedated only by those of Williams, the University of Virginia, and Princeton. It was founded in 1839 in the law office of Richard Yates, 1835, later to become governor of Illinois. It was established "for the purpose of mutual improvement and of the perpetuating the feelings and friendships of collegiate life."

During President Charles Henry Rammelkamp's administration, the idea that alumni should support their alma mater began to take hold. Dr. Rammelkamp persuaded his wife's brother, Dr. Edward Capps '87, a professor at Princeton, to promote a giving plan to be called the Alumni Fund. It was a scheme to raise money for endowment, not for current expenditures. Alumni would fund their permanent memberships by paying in $100 to the alumni endowment. The returns from their investment would become an annual contribution in perpetuity, and their names would be listed as annual contributors to the College forever. So strong was the idea that Alumni Fund money was for endowment only that when concerned alumni at the time of President Selden sought funds to "save the College" they did not use the Alumni Fund as the mechanism for solicitation but set up another organization.

During the troubled years just before my arrival, there had been tension between the trustees and alumni officials. Some years before, Jeanette Capps Rammelkamp, widow of the former president, had been alumni secretary. She had dominated alumni work and was succeeded by Mrs. Doris Dillon '20, a devoted and able person. When tensions developed, Mrs. Dillon was in an impossible situation because it was not clear whether she was responsible to the administration or to the alumni board. A strong faction of alumni leadership was opposed to Selden and at odds with the trustees. Mrs. Dillon was thought to lean in that direction also.

Before I found time to go into the problem, Mrs. Dillon resigned. Working in the alumni office was Mrs. Patricia Carlson Damsgaard '53, who wanted to remain at the College while her GI Bill husband, Conrad, finished his work for a degree in 1957. She was a very able person and was willing to be acting director for a year. That gave us time to work out a permanent solution to that problem.

The most significant indication that the College had entered a new era was the fact that the year-end report for 1955–1956 showed that the budget had been balanced for the first time since 1950. While I had some direct part in raising the necessary funds to achieve what was regarded as a near miracle, this accomplishment was more the result of other factors. Chief among them was a special campaign for funds headed by E. Dwight Smith '31, a Bell Telephone Company executive. Making use of his available free telephone service, he contacted people all over the country for money. Others on his committee spent much time in persuading people to help the College in a time of special need. Their efforts were sufficient to provide the extra money to meet all expenses. Here was the first of an unbroken series of balanced budgets that were to stretch beyond my administration. Smith received a richly deserved alumni citation for leading that effort.

By the end of the 1955–1956 academic year, College affairs were going better than I or anyone else had anticipated. Pat Damsgaard summed it up rather well in an editorial she wrote for the *Alumni Quarterly:*

The last few years have been difficult ones for Illinois College. There were some moments when we wondered if "the lamps our fathers lighted" would be extinguished. Illinois College is moving ahead.... Our new President shows an understanding of the College. He appreciates its heritage.... He has dedicated himself not to change for change's sake—but to build on the solid foundation of the past. The future looks bright—but much work remains.

During the early months of my relationship with Illinois College, I came to know and to have an enormous respect for

Genesis

the unusual people who comprised the trustees. They were a distinguished group, most of whom were alumni. Aside from three trustees nominated by the Alumni Association who served three-year overlapping terms and were not eligible for reelection immediately, there were twenty-one serving without term, including the president. There was one vacancy at that time, so there were twenty nonterm trustees when I arrived. Three of them were more than eighty years of age and three others over seventy-five; only two had been born in this century. One trustee was a woman. It was not strange that all but one trustee retired or died during my administration, and only one failed to resign before he lost his full mental powers.

And they were experienced! Eight had been trustees from thirty-one to forty-two years and two for more than twenty years. It is interesting to note that Dr. C. Ellsworth Black had succeeded his father as a trustee and that together they served a total of sixty-four years. Even more unusual was the fact that members of the Black family served on the board over a period of 124 years. The trustee who served the longest was Dr. George Baxter, former chairman, who resigned because of age after forty-two years.

One might think that this array of very successful people would be set in their ways and hard to deal with. This was not so. College affairs had gone badly of late, and the trustees were not anxious to second-guess a person they had brought in as an expert in the field of college administration. I often thought that the ablest among them had learned from experience in their own fields that expertise in one area, such as government or business, did not make a person an expert in education. They also were fully aware that changes had to take place in College procedures if the restoration they hoped for was to occur. Board members were anxious for strong leadership.

Without dissent, they all agreed that as individuals they would not involve themselves in administrative matters, in-

cluding faculty relations, except as prescribed in the bylaws. In this respect they never wavered. Years later, when a newly elected trustee took it upon himself to get involved in some administrative matters outside his field, a group of the old-timers informed him how things were done. I once was caught violating the very requirement I had insisted was necessary. I took a particularly knotty problem of an administrative nature to the board. Dr. Garm Norbury, the secretary and one of the wisest members, reminded me in his most gracious manner that this was an administrative matter, and it was up to me to handle it.

Since their beginnings, most Protestant colleges and all those related to the Presbyterian Church had required chapel services. In fact, in the earlier days, state universities had them also. In the 1950s, having regular, required chapel services and employing only members of evangelical Christian churches as faculty members were required in order to receive any denominational support. I fully concurred in the belief that the chapel requirement was a good thing. Roman Catholics could be exempted by bringing a written statement from their priests asking that they be excused.

At Illinois College, while the rule was enforced, a way had been found to circumvent it. Three absences were allowed each semester, and if more than that accumulated, the student was assessed a one dollar fine for each unexcused absence. In those days a dollar was a substantial amount of money. Some of the students who were not pressed for money had hit upon the idea of paying enough dollars at the opening of the semester and never bothering with chapel attendance. I regarded this sanctioned violation of the letter and spirit of the requirement to be intolerable and, at the annual meeting in June 1956, the trustees affirmed the requirement and abolished the forgiveness-for-money practice, which reminded me of the selling of indulgences.

Indications of the problems of the College and what lay ahead were stated in my annual report to the trustees at the

end of the 1955–1956 academic year, about five months after my arrival. The dining hall had been operating at a considerable loss for years, and it was illogical to continue subsidizing the feeding of students. The College was in the middle of a costly restoration of its buildings after years of inadequate maintenance. The new equipment for the Business Office would be installed by fall and all the irregular financial practices abolished. A plan to secure funds on a regular annual basis from alumni would be developed shortly. Faculty salaries must be raised substantially. It would be necessary to get some help for the president in the areas of public relations, alumni affairs, and development. The College was well on the way to better and closer relationships with the churches. It soon would be time to think about bringing into being the long-projected new chapel. This was the time to emphasize teacher education. Steps were being taken to involve the faculty more in student activities to overcome the morale problem within the student body and to improve such activities as the yearbook. The last two sentences in the report read as follows: "It seems to me that Illinois College stands at a moment of great opportunity. The question is whether or not we have the wisdom and the courage to grasp that opportunity."

The peace and lovely tranquility of summer on the beautiful campus was broken during the first and second summers by the noise of sandblasting and tuckpointing of all the old buildings. The campus Eden was not without its serpent. Old Jones Chapel had lost most of its bric-a-brac and small turrets, which had fallen to the ground and were buried by the ivy that almost covered the building. The ivy was grown from cuttings from Yale, which in turn had been transplanted from Oxford University. To their sorrow and pain, the workers discovered that the prolific growth of academic ivy had been infested with the poisonous variety. That, too, was eradicated.

2
The New Administration Takes Shape: 1956–1960

How much the disruptions and uncertainties of the recent past would affect the enrollment for the fall of 1956 was cause for some anxiety as the summer waned. While there was little prospect that enrollment would be increased substantially so soon, a further decline in numbers would be an ominous signal. It turned out that there was an increase and, although it was slight, it was a step in the right direction.

What had added to the uncertainty about enrollment was a change in admission standards. The previous fall, with enrollment promising to be so low that the life of the College was threatened, the normal admissions standards had been suspended and almost every person who applied was admitted. What to do about requirements for entrance in 1956 was one of the decisions that had to be made early in my administration.

At the strong urging of Dean Hildner and in spite of the dire need for greater enrollment, I concurred that if the institution was to be a good college it must have able students. The standards agreed upon and immediately put into effect were that students would be admitted routinely if they were in the upper half of their high-school graduating classes and if they were above a certain score on one of the standard achievement tests. Applicants not qualifying would have their records examined and the decision made by the Faculty Committee on Admissions.

This difficult but highly important decision turned out to

The Administration Takes Shape

be a signal that Illinois College was to continue as it had been traditionally, a strong academic institution worthy of its Phi Beta Kappa chapter. The committee refused admission to forty applicants that fall. The question of presidential interference with admissions is a lively one for small colleges. I recall one of my fellow presidents telling me that he reserved the right to override the admissions committee at his institution. Another president allowed himself the privilege of admitting a certain small number without referring them to the admission committee. I resolved to keep free of the admissions process and to rely wholly on the faculty committee to handle marginal cases. This is not to say that attempts were not made to get me to overrule the committee.

On numerous occasions, ministers, financial supporters, and even members of the board intervened on behalf of sons or daughters of friends. Almost always the interveners believed the prospective students had good grades when the opposite was true. I always got the facts and informed interveners why applicants were denied admission and added that it was a service to these persons to be turned down because, were they admitted, they would fail. If prospective students really thought they could do college work, they had better enroll at one of the state colleges where the going would be easier. Not the least of our troubles had to do with zealous sports followers who believed that superior athletic ability should be regarded more highly than ability to achieve academically. The committee treated athletes exactly as they did other students.

One of the serious problems for years had been the difficulty of collecting student charges. Every year, considerable sums in unpaid bills from former students had to be written off. The practice of admitting students to classes on the simple assumption that the bills could be settled later had to be changed.

During the previous semester a plan had been worked out

and all families had been informed that arrangements for paying college bills would have to be made before a student would be admitted to classes. Families who needed credit so charges could be paid in installments were referred to Tuition Plan, a credit organization that was in effect a private lending agency of national scope that would advance the college whatever the student owed and get its money back with interest on the installment plan. Thus, every student before going to classes had made final arrangements for payment or had already paid for the semester.

The trustees were surprised when I reported at the end of registration that two-thirds of the first semester bills were fully paid and that valid agreements had been negotiated for receiving the rest of the money before the middle of the semester. It is to be remembered that no state or federal aid plans were in effect at that time except for the GI Bill, which still benefited a few men.

The first trustee that I had an opportunity to nominate was elected by the board in 1956. He was Dr. Harold Martin, pastor of the Second Presbyterian Church of Bloomington and one of the leaders of the denomination. Within a year, he was elected moderator of the General Assembly, the church's highest office. As a result, the College had on its board at the same time the leaders of two major denominations, the other being Chairman Fred Hoskins.

The semester opened with a full-time faculty of twenty-eight and some part-time instructors. Of the twenty-eight, thirteen were new to the College and another four were beginning their second year. As a result, it was easier to make changes in the way things were to be done but harder for the dean and the president to make the operation go smoothly.

On October 19, 1956, a glorious autumn day with the campus awash with brightly colored leaves, the new president was inaugurated. In the procession were the representatives of more than 150 colleges and universities in the order of their founding with Harvard (1636) leading the way, followed

The Administration Takes Shape

President Caine and Dr. Fred Hoskins, chairman of the Board of Trustees, in the inauguration procession.

by Yale, Pennsylvania, Princeton, and Columbia. Last in line was the president of Roosevelt University, founded in 1945. Some twenty representatives of learned societies and educational and religious organizations followed. Exercises were held in Memorial Gymnasium, board chairman Fred Hoskins presiding. Greetings were brought by leaders of various related organizations at the inauguration or at the luncheon that followed. The chief speaker was President Charles Turck of Macalester College. After the luncheon, a public reception was held at our home. It was a memorable day.

During the year, the new dormitory for women was under construction and the athletic field was being graded and tiled. By the following fall, all the renovations of buildings had essentially been completed.

The Caine sons, Stanley, Alan, and Clifford, Elizabeth Caine, and Mrs. Charles Rammelkamp listen to the inaugural address.

When travel was restricted during World War II, the traditional baccalaureate and commencement exercises had been combined. The war never ended as far as baccalaureate was concerned and only commencement exercises had been held for more than a dozen years. Since Illinois College probably was the only church-related college in the nation without a baccalaureate service, I recommended that it be restored to the activities of Commencement Week. The restoration took place in 1957 with trustee and moderator of the General Assembly of the Presbyterian Church, Harold Martin, as the preacher. Baccalaureate was held on Sunday morning and Commencement the next day.

One incident from the annual meeting of the trustees has stuck in my mind. For many years the College had found it necessary to borrow money to pay bills throughout the summer during the days of unbalanced budgets. The customary motion allowing borrowing of up to $50,000 during the

The Administration Takes Shape

summer was made. I suggested that I did not think any borrowing would be necessary. One of the oldest members spoke up sharply, saying, "I don't believe it!" In deference to him, the motion was passed. No borrowing took place, however, and it was the last time such a motion was offered.

Also, at the annual meeting, in spite of somewhat strained relations with MacMurray, the board, by a special resolution, saluted the new MacMurray College for Men and wished them well.

The College received some national publicity when *Presbyterian Life,* the official magazine of the Presbyterian Church, was persuaded to send a representative and write a story that appeared in June 1957. The article "Campus in Lincolnland," occupied more than four pages, with a cover picture of Mignon DuBois, a student of the College who also was a member of the Westminster Fellowship National Council.

By the beginning of classes in the fall of 1957, even the pessimistic agreed that this was the threshold of a new era. The new MacMurray College for Men had opened and, in spite of their substantial subsidies to induce men to enroll at what had been a women's college, the enrollment at Illinois College went up for the second year and continued to do so at a satisfactory rate. The College had experienced two years of balanced operating budgets after six successive years of deficits. In 1956, it was in the black only by some $10,000. In 1956–1957, the surplus was about $38,000 in spite of large expenditures to bring the neglected plant up to standard and to provide substantial salary increases.

The modernization and total reorganization of the business operations of the College had been accomplished, and a new business manager was in charge. Another administrative change brought to the campus Leonard Wilson, a young man who had completed his hitch in the navy after brief employment at his alma mater, Hastings College. He had used his GI Bill benefits to secure a master's degree at Boston Univer-

sity and was appointed alumni secretary and Director of Public Relations under rather special circumstances.

Pat Damsgaard, after receiving her degree in 1953, had stayed on in Jacksonville as part-time acting alumni secretary while her husband completed his work for a degree. Now they planned to move to Chicago where he was to be employed. I was desperately overloaded with administrative duties. Because the job of alumni secretary was hardly more than half-time, the balance of Wilson's time could be employed in other administrative duties.

While it was only logical for an alumnus to be the alumni secretary, there was a good reason why it was better to appoint an outsider this time. Alumni board members had been at odds with the trustees over various issues before my coming; to appoint someone from outside was a convenient way of avoiding further trouble.

At this time of transition, there was a real need for some added means of communicating with supporters of the College. I envisioned a small monthly house-organ written entirely by the president to inform the constituency about the problems and intentions of the College. It would help to build good will and promote giving. Since the budget would not stand the cost of such a publication, I sought a sponsor. State Senator James D. Monroe '13, editor and publisher of the *Collinsville Herald*, happily agreed to publish such a bulletin four times each year as a contribution to the College. Thus, *Comments* came into being. When Monroe's son, Karl '37, succeeded him, the arrangement continued. It was a most valuable gift.

Over the years, many gifts in kind came to the College, mostly as a result of our suggestions. Among them was all the surveying for new buildings, legal services, surfacing of parking lots and tennis courts, furniture, books, paper products, lectures, teaching help, trees, and shrubs. Donors seemed to get special satisfaction in gifts of a more personal nature.

The Administration Takes Shape

One of the most valuable training experiences for both Elizabeth and me took place in the summer of 1957, when we were selected to attend without expense a ten-day seminar for new college presidents at Harvard University. Sponsored by the Association of American Colleges and financed by the Carnegie Foundation, it brought together twenty-five beginning presidents. Using the famous case method of the Harvard Business School, the group went over difficult administrative matters that might be encountered in the days ahead. The wives studied their roles also.

The new presidents were from institutions of all sizes, including the universities of Colorado, North Carolina, and Nebraska. It was interesting to see how they did in their jobs in later years. A number did not succeed but some rose to great heights of leadership. One was Clifford Hardin, the new chancellor of the University of Nebraska, who later became secretary of agriculture in the Nixon cabinet and then vice-chairman of the board of Ralston Purina.

To overcome some of the negative ideas concerning the College that had developed during the troubled times, we took special pains to enhance the institution's image. When we discovered that *Who's Who in America* ranked Illinois College twenty-sixth in the nation in the percentage of its graduates listed in the current issue, we gave it wide publicity. It was especially impressive to know that for the state, Illinois College ranked first, with Knox and the University of Chicago tied for second.

Another fact we used then and in succeeding years was that certain families had long associations with the College. The student body had three prime examples that year. Kay Milligan's father and mother both were members of the Class of 1925, while her grandfather had graduated in 1897, and a great-uncle in 1869. John Badger was the son of a member of the Class of 1929; his aunt, Ruth Badger Pixley '18, was a trustee of the College. Her sister had attended the Jacksonville Female Academy and John's great-great-grandmother

had attended it in 1838. Steve Ramsey's brother preceded him, and his great-grandfather was a faculty member of the Medical School that had been on the campus in the 1840s. Another relative was Dr. Hiram Jones, a member of the faculty from 1869 to 1903, and the donor of the money for Jones Hall.

When we first saw the president's house on the Illinois College campus, we were struck by the fact that in size and elegance it rivaled those of much larger institutions. That such a grand place had been erected about the turn of the century for a tiny, struggling college was explained only by the fact that President Clifford Webster Barnes was a wealthy man who built the house as his contribution to a financial campaign that failed. He left; the house remained. The furnishings were priceless as well. Most were from the Gardner estate, including Chinese pieces and oriental rugs. The house was a veritable showplace.

We were a little self-conscious about it and began to look for ways that the house would be of more use to the College. We decided to make it a center of culture and education for students, faculty, and the community. Elizabeth was a willing and able hostess, and her contributions to the presidency were of the highest order. We entertained groups of students and faculty at teas, receptions, and meals. Women's organizations and community groups met there. We entertained more than three thousand people each year. Elizabeth kept careful notes of each meeting so that if it were repeated the following year she would know how many to expect and what should be done—including how many cookies had to be available.

Having lived for some years in a metropolis that was a great cultural center and having been connected with a college with a strong bent toward international relations, it appeared to us that Jacksonville was a bit isolated. We determined that among the things we wished to do was to help broaden the horizons of students as well as citizens of

The Administration Takes Shape

Jacksonville. Our first effort was to inaugurate a series of lectures by distinguished visitors, including not only people of other races and cultures but leaders in science, religion, culture, and the arts. Since the financial condition of the College precluded any appreciable budget for this purpose, we resolved to get these visitors on a contribution basis. Some people came at their own expense, and others were sponsored by corporations and foundations.

The plan we usually followed was to have the visitor arrive on Sunday afternoon. He or she often used the Baxter Hall guest apartment. Activities would begin with a Sunday evening session at our home. Some fifty or sixty people from the community would be invited. The guest would make an opening statement related to his or her work or position and then would answer questions for an hour. After refreshments and when everyone had had an opportunity to meet the visitor, the evening was concluded.

Convocations were held on Monday mornings with the guest as speaker. He or she would also lead discussions in two or three classes. In the case of persons of greater renown, there would be a press conference and interviews for radio and television. In some cases we would have a joint meeting of Jacksonville area service clubs to hear the visitor. At times, arrangements would be made to have half-hour interviews on the Springfield or Quincy television stations, and sometimes our visitor would speak to service clubs in Springfield. The visit of Melvin Laird, when he was secretary of defense, was covered by the national television networks.

Aside from the people who came to the College as a result of this program, there was the annual Phi Beta Kappa lecturer, a highlight of the intellectual season. Another fine cultural attraction for many years was the annual appearance of a string quartet, which at first was financed by a foundation and later by an anonymous donor and subscription. Most of the best quartets in the nation and those in residence at major universities took their turns.

Aside from some of our trustees and alumni of prominence, in the first year the visitors included Bishop Stephen Neill of the Church of England, former general secretary of the World Council of Churches; the moderator of the Presbyterian General Assembly; Dr. Marcus Bach of the School of Religion, University of Iowa; the author Paul Engle; and the senior editor of the *Reader's Digest,* Stanley High.

The visit of the latter was an example of a corporate gift. I had had previous contacts with DeWitt Wallace, owner and publisher of the *Reader's Digest,* whose father had been president of Macalester College many years before. I sought support for Illinois College from him without much success, but he promised to supply us with some of his people as distinguished visitors at his expense. We had a number of senior editors and others including Stanley High, Charles Ferguson, and former congressman and medical missionary, Walter Judd. Later on, I did get $12,500 as a student aid endowment.

We took no-cost distinguished visitors wherever we could find them. An example is one who seemed to come by chance. I was returning on a plane from New York and found myself seated next to a man who wanted to talk. It turned out that he was a high official of the Bell Telephone Company. He expressed his deep interest in private colleges and left himself open by saying his company was happy to help colleges in any way it could. I told him I had something in mind that Bell Telephone could do for us: send us a good scientist for about two days. He said he would see what he could do. Within a week, I had a letter from him saying that Dr. Raymond Ketchledge, executive director of the Bell Laboratories and one of the developers of the proximity fuse, so important in World War II, would spend two days with us.

Before launching the Distinguished Visitors Program, it had been necessary to arrange another period for the student body to assemble. As previously noted, the trustees had reaffirmed required chapel, but chapel, so called, had gotten to

The Administration Takes Shape

be more often a meeting rather than a religious service. While some chapel sessions were worship services, others were pep meetings or other types of nonreligious programs. At my request, the trustees established a convocation and a chapel period each week with the requirement that students attend both.

Convocation became an occasion where the college community shared a common experience. It included such programs as the finals of intersociety debates and other forensic activities, Honors convocation and an occasion to present athletic awards, the homecoming convocation, the president's address at the first convocation each semester, the introduction of new faculty members, and the discussion of campus programs or problems. High in importance was the opportunity to listen to distinguished visitors.

All institutions of higher learning, even the state universities, once had chapel services with mandatory attendance. Religion was considered an essential part of education. It was impossible to think of the church relationship without knowing that all students would be required to go to daily chapel services.

Nearly all the institutions of higher learning in the early days of America were church colleges. Harvard, the first, was founded in 1636 by Congregationalists for the purpose of training ministers to take the place of those who had come over from England when they would "lie in the dust." In nearly all the states east of the Mississippi, the first colleges were church related. It was not until the Morrill Act was signed by Abraham Lincoln that federal financial assistance gave impetus to the founding of tax-supported institutions such as the University of Illinois.

Illinois College, first in the state to graduate a class, was founded by Presbyterians and Congregationalists under the Plan of Union. The plan divided up the territory to prevent competition and duplication of efforts. Illinois was Presbyterian territory so the College was under Presbyterian aus-

pices even though most of the members of the Yale Band were Congregationalists. The plan broke down because the Congregationalists did not like the central control of individual churches by Presbyteries or the tests of orthodoxy imposed by the Presbyterian system. Even some of the leaders at Illinois College were tried for their beliefs, and so Congregationalists in the town of Jacksonville rebelled and started the Congregational Church of Jacksonville, one of the earliest in Illinois.

By the mid-1800s, the College was related to a Congregational denomination composed of autonomous local churches without a central creed and with no denominational financial support. The Presbyterians supplied money and required conformity to certain standards. In the 1950s, these standards included required chapel, study of the Bible as a part of the curriculum, and the stipulation that the faculty be members of an evangelical Christian church. At that time, almost all denominations had some such requirements for their colleges.

President H. Gary Hudson and others at Illinois College clashed with leaders of the Board of Christian Education of the Presbyterian Church over some of its requirements. The trustees became concerned that the College might be removed from Presbyterian auspices and took steps to bring about a reconciliation. Their first move was taken when Harry J. Dunbaugh '99 resigned the chairmanship of the board in 1955, and a leading clergyman, Dr. Fred Hoskins, took his place as chairman. Although a Congregationalist, Hoskins enjoyed good relations with the Presbyterian powers. The next move was to appoint a chaplain. Since there was no money to bring in another faculty member, arrangements were made to employ the Reverend Joseph Baus, pastor of the First Presbyterian Church, on a part-time basis. When the board selected a new president who had been a lay leader of some importance in the Presbyterian Church, the troubles were over. The following year, the Congregational Church

The Administration Takes Shape

supplied the money to employ a full-time chaplain and religion teacher.

As time went on, the Presbyterian Church removed all its requirements for continuing affiliation. It lost almost all its interest in colleges and provided them only token support. The saddest development of my years as a churchman was the almost complete lack of genuine concern on the part of the two related denominations for their colleges. They still pay lip service to their responsibility, but it goes little beyond that.

The twenty-fifth anniversary of the installation of a Phi Beta Kappa chapter on the Illinois College campus was marked by special recognitions in 1957. Dr. Mortimer Smith presented a lecture entitled "The Diminished Mind," and Dr. W. T. Hastings, president of the United Chapters, was the featured speaker at the anniversary banquet.

During the academic year of 1957–1958, three outstanding faculty members who had served the College for thirty years were honored. Each was a person of strong convictions, an outstanding teacher who would serve the College for some years to come, and a significant figure in the community. President Charles Henry Rammelkamp had hired them nearly all at the same time. His wise choices were to benefit the College with a combined total of some hundred years of service of the very highest quality. They served during the tenure of five of the ten presidents. Professor Earle B. Miller (mathematics) was appointed first and his wife, Dr. Eleanor O. Miller (psychology), next. While all began teaching at the same time, Dr. Joe Patterson Smith (history)—to his chagrin—had to be satisfied with being third in seniority.

After the Centennial effort, which produced Tanner Library and Baxter Hall in 1927, nothing was added to the campus but World War II surplus buildings until 1950, when Memorial Gymnasium, named in honor of those who served in the war, was constructed. The building was planned to be

much larger but not enough money could be raised; only a basketball court with room for spectators and a basement providing dressing rooms, showers, and a rifle range were built. An expansive slab to the north lacked a roof. The doors in the south wall led nowhere.

When the HHFA came into being at about the beginning of the decade, Illinois College began to consider building a new dormitory. The College was granted a loan of $200,000 to construct a dormitory for men with most of the lower floor set aside for a student union. This sum was insufficient so the trustees agreed to the dubious action of borrowing $100,000 from the endowment to pay the rest of the cost. Later on, they discovered that they had to borrow another $14,000 for furnishings. No provision was made to pay back the endowment. The dormitory, later named Gardner Hall, was completed in 1954.

To make matters worse, there was no prospect of having another 100 men to fill the new dormitory. The enrollment was actually decreasing. When I arrived, the hall was but partly filled. Its gross income was $15,000; its current operating costs $10,000, and repayment of principal and interest another $9,000—a loss of $4,000 for the year.

When the men moved into the new dormitory, Crampton was left empty and a generous friend of the College provided the money to refurbish it for a women's residence. Soon after the opening of college in 1955, at a time when there was no president, the trustees made application for a loan to build a dormitory for women. There really was no need for the building unless enrollment increased greatly. In 1954–1955, there were only sixty full-time women students, a number of whom were commuters. Besides Crampton Hall, which accommodated all the women seeking campus housing, Fayerweather House was available; and Colonial Inn had been rented to the hospital because it was not needed by the College. Fortunately, by the time the new women's dormitory was ready for occupancy in the fall of 1957, enrollment had improved sub-

The Administration Takes Shape

stantially; it was likely that student housing would soon become a self-liquidating budget item.

The dedication of the new dormitory for women was an especially historic occasion. While women had been included in the student body for some fifty years, this was the first building erected for the exclusive use of women in the history of the College. The first stirring of the women's movement fueled the enthusiasm of the alumnae who were a distinct minority in the Alumni Association. Under the leadership of Mrs. Beatrice Hartman '34 and Mrs. Carol Lohman '45, alumnae raised $22,000 to furnish the new building in a campaign called "Operation Co-Ed." The principal speaker for the dedication was Congressman Sid Simpson, who had helped with the application for federal funds.

With the full concurrence of the women students, the dormitory was named Ellis Hall in memory of the Reverend John Ellis and his wife Frances, who not only were responsible for the founding of the College but who also established a school for girls at the same time. This school became the Jacksonville Female Academy, which, when united with the College in 1903, made the College coeducational.

At the beginning of my administration, there was plenty of classroom space. Biology and chemistry were taught in Sturtevant Hall and physics in Whipple Hall. Jones Hall was a classroom building, and a few classes were held in Russell House. Most of the nonscience departments met in Federal Hall, a World War II surplus building. The literary societies had ample rooms also. The women divided the space in Smith House, and the men's societies met in Beecher Hall and Russell House.

It is interesting to trace the building program through my years at Illinois College. For almost the whole time, building and renovation were going on. Except for the dormitories, which were built with low-cost, self-liquidating federal loans, everything was paid with money raised at the time and without federal grants. By the fall of 1960, more living quarters

were needed for both men and women. Men were living in Gardner and Crampton, and women needed more than Ellis and Fayerweather. Another HHFA loan made it possible to more than double the capacity of Ellis to 114 in the fall of 1962.

In the spring of 1961, the cornerstone was laid for Rammelkamp Chapel. It was completed and dedicated in April 1962. A month later, ground was broken for Crispin Science Hall, and it was dedicated at Commencement in 1963. During the academic year 1963–1964, the swimming pool addition to Memorial Gymnasium was completed.

In 1964, another HHFA loan was negotiated to build another men's dormitory and an addition to the dining hall. Both of these facilities were put to use in the fall of 1965. The dormitory was named for Jonathan Baldwin Turner.

Sturtevant Hall stood vacant for two years after the science departments were moved into Crispin Hall in 1963. The need for more classroom and office space required its renovation for the second time. In 1920 it had been gutted by fire and remodeled for a science hall after serving as an all-purpose building earlier. Its current renovation provided eleven additional classrooms, a number of faculty offices, and quarters for Pi Pi Rho, a men's society.

When Rammelkamp Chapel was completed, the former chapel-auditorium in Jones was transformed into a theater, using an anteroom to the south as the stage; the spectator seating was tiered upward as in a stadium because the stage could not be elevated. An incident in connection with that remodeling bears recounting.

It became necessary to get new seats for the theater. We learned that a movie theater in Litchfield was being renovated and that the used seats were for sale. It was November 22, 1963, when Mrs. Caine and I drove off in a pelting rain to have a look at the seats to see if they were suitable for our theater. (We purchased the seats and had them reupholstered.) At a filling station in Springfield we heard the shock-

ing news that President Kennedy had been shot in Dallas. All the way down and back we listened to the unfolding story of one of the most dramatic days in recent history—the death of Kennedy and the elevation of Lyndon B. Johnson to power.

When Crispin Science Hall was built, physics and mathematics were taught in Whipple Hall. When they were moved into the new science hall, Whipple was remodeled for the Admissions Department and Placement Bureau, along with the offices of the Education Department. When Tanner Library began to overflow, the unused books and old bound periodicals were stored in the top floor of Whipple.

By 1964 it became obvious that more housing for women would be required. Another HHFA loan was arranged and in the fall of 1966 Pixley Hall was opened.

The GI Bill enrollment bulge in 1947 had necessitated bringing in a surplus army camp building known as Federal Hall. It was deteriorating and the unused lower floor of Rammelkamp Chapel was divided into classrooms and Federal was demolished in 1965.

The student center was opened in 1967. To my boundless surprise, in 1976, three years after my retirement, it was named for me.

In addition to buildings, parking lots, tennis courts, new sidewalks, and other improvements were added during my tenure as president. Most important of these projects was the development of the outdoor athletic facilities, the baseball diamond, and the football field with its added facilities.

Of much more than passing importance was the return of Dr. Charles Frank to the Illinois College faculty. He came to the College first in 1939 as an instructor in English, then obtained his doctorate from Princeton University, spent the war years in the navy on leave of absence, and became chairman of the English Department. During the turmoil of the Selden administration, like so many others, he resigned. It was reported that he was unhappy with his position at the University of Nevada and wished he were back at Illinois

College. I had never met him, but everybody spoke of him as a superior teacher and colleague. After carefully checking to be sure he was not a disturber of the peace and that his former students, the trustees, and the people of the community thought him an asset to the College, we invited him to rejoin the faculty. It was an important decision, and his superior services to the College and to the community made him a significant figure for many years.

Among the factors that had to be considered in inviting him to return was his status on the faculty. He had been co-chairman of the department with Dr. Ethel Seybold. She expressed a desire to have him return and graciously suggested that he again be made co-chairman. We complied with her wishes, and the two colleagues once again presided over one of the College's strongest areas.

Another able teacher, Ruth Bump, joined the English Department and remained through my administration and beyond.

The rapidly improving financial condition of the College had been reflected in faculty salaries. Salaries had reached the top of the supposedly dangerously high new salary schedule of two years before and a new one was adopted. A report of the United States Office of Education then showed that in only one rank were salaries below the average for colleges of that size over the nation. That year, also, a very popular faculty benefit was added. A charitable trust in Chicago was induced to make the first of a series of annual grants to pay the expenses of faculty members to attend meetings of learned societies. When the grant expired three years later, that item was picked up in the regular budget. The fund was administered by a faculty committee.

When I discovered that a son of William Jennings Bryan (Class of 1881), the College's best known graduate, lived in San Francisco, I asked him if there were any books, papers, or mementos of his father which he would like to give to the College. He sent several books and another item of rare inter-

The Administration Takes Shape

Carl Robinson '09 *(right)* and President Caine examine a book and track medal of William Jennings Bryan, Class of 1881.

est. It was a medal his father had received for winning the standing broad jump at a college meet. Engraved on the back was the distance, 12 feet and 4 inches. Although that event is no longer contested, it did seem to be a good distance.

All along I had been deeply involved in leadership roles in the two related denominations. I had been an active layman in the Presbyterian Church for many years but the other denomination also required attention. The College had a time-honored relationship with the Congregational Churches that were co-founders of the College. They had merged with the Christian Church to form the Congregational Christian

Church. In 1957, another merger with the Evangelical and Reformed Church formed the United Church of Christ.

The Presbyterian Church had divided into Northern and Southern Churches over slavery, and Illinois College had naturally remained connected with the northern group, called the Presbyterian Church in the United States of America. Still another branch of Presbyterianism was the United Presbyterian Church. A merger of that group and the Presbyterian Church to which Illinois College was related formed the United Presbyterian Church in the United States.

At the beginning of my administration, four colleges in the state were related to the Presbyterian Church U.S.A.—Blackburn, Millikin, Lake Forest, and Illinois. The merger with the United Presbyterian Church added Monmouth to the list.

In the old Congregationalist days, Knox and Rockford Colleges had been related to that denomination. Both had fallen away and did not renew their church ties. Elmhurst College had been related to the Evangelical Church, and the second merger of the Congregational side made Elmhurst and Illinois sister institutions in the United Church of Christ.

All this merging required a lot of meetings and conferences. I was one of four presidents of colleges of the United Church to work out the relationship of colleges to the church. On the Presbyterian side, I spent even more time, serving on a committee that established the National Presbyterian Scholarship program, chairing the Synod's Committee on Church Related Colleges, and serving as a trustee of the Synod.

While all these duties required a great deal of time, the work was worth doing. As a churchman, I thought it was my duty to help out, but I also believed that it was to the advantage of Illinois College to have its president identified with the forward movement of two great denominations.

In the fall of 1957, when the trustees met, the mood was optimistic. When I had been appointed less than two years earlier, the board had no idea that the situation at the College

The Administration Takes Shape

could possibly be so greatly improved in such a short time. The financial crisis had been almost completely resolved, and the future seemed promising. The board expressed its deep appreciation in a formal resolution and, at my suggestion, authorized the transfer of $32,000 from current fund surplus to the endowment. This was the first step in the total restoration of all the endowment funds that had been used for current operations over previous years.

So confident was the board that the College would move ahead that for the first time in my administration there was talk about new buildings. The Development Committee, which had not met for years, was instructed to convene and to bring to the spring meeting some recommendations for moving ahead.

Donald Funk, president of Sangamo Electric in Springfield, was chairman of the Development Committee. He was host to the committee at a luncheon at his club in Springfield, an event that turned out to be a historic occasion. The committee listened to a rather detailed report of the president on the financial condition and prospects of the College. This and a later report to the full board became the blueprints for the future development of the College that were followed for the next twenty years.

In the report, I expressed the opinion that faculty salaries would have to be increased substantially and that other costs would climb. Prospective increases in enrollment, a better response from donors, and a gradual increase in tuition would assure a balanced operating budget. Endowment would be increased substantially, mainly from wills and bequests, which must be skillfully promoted. To make it easier to get financial commitments in wills, it was essential to adopt a policy that every bequest, unless otherwise designated by the maker, would go into the endowment and never be used for any current purpose. It was at that time that the board adopted a schedule to repay the $114,000 of endowment money which had been used for the construction of

Gardner Hall and to pay the endowment fund annual interest on the unpaid balance.

By the trustees' meeting in the spring of 1958, we had developed a master plan, called the Forward Step, for the years ahead. It was first necessary to determine the enrollment for which provisions should be made. The figure of 800 was agreed upon. There were some who wanted to make it higher but for a college with an enrollment of half that size and with the experience of having dipped below 300, most of the trustees supported that figure. The price of the total expansion was not calculated, and the first financial goal for buildings was set at $1,500,000. This sum was much more than the College had ever set out to raise, and it was regarded as about as big a bite as could be chewed. It was decided at the same time that no building would be commenced without having funds for its construction at hand except dormitories where income paid off construction loans.

The next decision had to do with the priorities for new construction. It was not difficult to get agreement on building the chapel first. It had been proposed more than thirty years before, and there was even a small fund to go toward its construction. Next would come a science hall and then a swimming pool addition to the gymnasium. When the sciences were moved out of Sturtevant Hall, that building would be remodeled and so would Whipple Hall. What had been the chapel room in Jones Hall would then be more adequately fitted for a little theater. There were other tasks to be done, but the projected $1,500,000 fund to be raised would only cover the first few. It was understood that the first campaign would have to be followed by others. Then, too, there was no pressing need for all these new buildings; as the enrollment grew, facilities would keep pace with the enlargement of the student body.

In retrospect, that plan adopted so long ago turned out to be better than we knew at the time. It is quite remarkable that all of it was eventually carried out. Even the enrollment

figure was a good one. It is true that for a few years the gross exceeded that number and even reached a high of 920, but this size did not hold. After my retirement, it took some effort to maintain an enrollment of 800. It was most fortunate that we did not opt for an unobtainable figure as so many colleges did to their sorrow.

Having boldly set out a figure of $1,500,000 to be raised, how to reach it became the issue. Never before had the College had a campaign for more than $200,000, and history recorded more failures than successes in these efforts. I was an experienced and successful fund raiser, but there was much merit in the argument that I had my hands full with other aspects of reordering the affairs of the College. Some help for a major fund campaign was required. The College had not had good experiences with professional fund raisers and I had no enthusiasm for them, but no better source of help was in sight. We decided to use professional services.

At the appointed time, the company sent in a director for the effort. While he was of some help in setting up the organization, he offended many people. His work proved to be so ineffective that at the end of the prescribed period, when the contract would have been renewed, we paid off the company and went on without outside help. I directed the financial campaigns for the rest of my administration.

Dormitory directors are key people on any campus, and not many are suited for these positions. There was a school of thought that said that these persons should be trained in counseling and guidance. My experience had been that older women with a real interest in young people are more likely to be successful than younger professionals. "Housemothers," as we called them then, is a description of what good dormitory directors are. Sometimes it was hard to find the right people close at hand.

Presbyterian Life, the official publication of the Presbyterian Church, ran an article about the need for older people to help in carrying out the mission of the church. It told of

various volunteer opportunities overseas and at home. I wrote a letter, which was published, saying that the article left out a very important area of service—that of being housemothers at church-related colleges. The pay was not good but the service opportunities were limitless.

The response to the letter was overwhelming. Women from all over the nation wrote to inquire how they might go about locating such a position. I replied to all their letters, suggesting the names of colleges near them to which they might apply. We still needed someone at Illinois College. One woman in particular stood out above most of the others. She was Mrs. Louise Becker, formerly of Illinois but now living in the East. I arranged to meet her when I went to New York and hired her.

Mrs. Becker was a very able and dedicated person who served during the rest of my administration and beyond. She was hired at a very low salary, but through all the years she never accepted a raise and gave back to the College, largely through dormitory improvements, more than she was paid. She made a lasting impact on the boys she supervised, and, at her retirement, they held a reunion in her honor and placed a plaque honoring her in the Crampton lounge.

About this time, the College received a unique gift from a man who had become famous in the world of business. Roger Babson attracted international attention when he correctly predicted the stock-market crash of 1929. His Babson Institute and writings on business and economics kept him in the public eye. He was a leading Congregational layman and had held the elected leadership of the church for a term not long before this incident.

As the president of a Congregational Church related college, I was a delegate to the annual national assembly of the church. Before the gathering that year in Boston, I had asked to have a talk with him. He responded by inviting me to lunch on the first day. I had visions of going to a posh club at noon, but instead he took me to a fast food outlet where we had a

The Administration Takes Shape

hotdog as the main course. Thrift may have had something to do with his financial status.

I told him of the financial needs of Illinois College and how we were trying to get it back on track. I expressed the hope that he would help us. He replied that he was doing all he could for higher education. He supported the Babson Institute and two other educational institutions. One was a high-grade school, run by his niece, that trained women to be assistants to top business executives. He encouraged me to visit it, which I later did. Babson feared that the Soviet Union was preparing to blast the United States with nuclear bombs. In that event, the East Coast would be ruined so he was establishing a new college in Kansas, the least likely place to be bombed.

But he had a way of contibuting which he said the trustees would not accept. (Babson took a dim view of college trustees, saying that they were shortsighted and timid about their endowment investments.) He would give the College the equivalent of a million dollars if the trustees were willing to do what he prescribed. He then illustrated what he had in mind.

When he married his wife some fifty years before, she was a school teacher with less than $5,000 in assets. He told her that he would provide for all her needs and desires and also make her a millionaire. He took her assets and invested them. They had grown to nearly $6 million in value.

He proposed to give Illinois College $12,500 to be invested and not touched for sixty-seven years, by which time it would grow to be more than $1 million. The money would be placed in the hands of a trustee agreeable to him. Managing fees would come from the earnings. The money was to be invested in Canadian mining stocks costing less than two dollars per share; whenever a stock doubled in value or declared its first dividend, it had to be sold and another one bought.

Babson said that most of these cheap stocks never

amounted to anything, but those who issued them profited greatly when they became worthless. Usually they advanced in price rapidly at first and sometimes they paid a dividend to induce investors to purchase them. One could make money fast by getting rid of them early in the game. He went on to say that he was about to go to Africa, and he would give the money and make the arrangements when he got back if our trustees were willing to take the gift as prescribed.

With no idea that this would amount to anything but with nothing to lose by accepting, the board agreed to take his gift and abide by his terms.

When Babson returned from Africa, he reported that he had changed his mind—he had a better investment. He predicted that the De Beers mining company, which had gone into chemicals, was destined to be the "DuPont of Africa." The money should be invested in De Beers or in its successors. We concurred and, when I retired in 1973, the $12,500 had grown to $207,400. I will not be around at the end of the sixty-seven years, but it is not unlikely that it will be worth more than $1 million.

One of the newly elected trustees who was later made a trustee without term was Robert Oxtoby '43, a Springfield attorney and former assistant U.S. district attorney. His late father had been a long time member of the College faculty.

As the College entered the decade of the 1960s, its gains were impressive. Enrollment in 1960 was twice as high as it had been at the low point of the 1950s. Ellis Hall had been constructed and old buildings had undergone major refurbishing inside and out. Money spent from the endowment had been restored, and the endowment had been increased by nearly three-quarters of a million dollars. Yearly gifts were ten times as much in 1960 as they had been in 1950, and the College was embarking on a new campaign of expansion.

One of the small miracles of the latter half of the decade of the 1950s was the dramatic reversal of the financial picture, and nothing better illustrates that than the condition of the

current fund. During the first half of the decade, unbalanced budgets resulted in a substantial deficit funded by the endowment. During the fiscal year in which I came to the College, the budget was balanced for the first time in the decade, but barely. Balanced budgets continued but by 1959-1960, income from the operation of the College and endowment income were sufficient to balance the budget without the use of a single cent of gift money. For the rest of my administration and beyond, no gift money was used for the operating budget. It all went into new buildings and improvements, new equipment, and the endowment.

Two of the most distinguished trustees, both men known nationwide, died that year. The first was James Barnes '2L, a former member of Congress and administrative assistant to both President Roosevelt and President Truman. The other was Benjamin Thomas, the distinguished Lincoln scholar and author. So highly regarded was he among writers and students of Lincoln's life and times that the Civil War Roundtable of Springfield took the lead in establishing a memorial for him. Because of his close connections with Illinois College and the College's role in the Lincoln era, they decided that the memorial would be on this campus. They raised a fund to provide an alcove in one end of the reading room of Tanner Library, furnished it with comfortable chairs and davenports, and supplied hundreds of books both new and old on the Civil War period. Plaques, Thomas's picture, and a special place for the books he had written were other features of the memorial. To dedicate the memorial and to speak at Commencement the next day, the Roundtable invited Thomas's friend and fellow author, Bruce Catton, editor of the *American Heritage* and Pulitzer Prize winner for his *Stillness at Appomattox*.

The Benjamin Thomas Memorial added much to an already significant collection of books and artifacts relating to Lincoln and the Civil War. In the president's office could be found Lincoln's office chair and on the wall—framed—an

original Lincoln letter. The chair was an object of interest to many. Sometimes entire busloads of schoolchildren would come, line up, come in one door of the office and go out the other, pausing to sit for a few seconds in Lincoln's chair.

At the Commencement, Catton gave an excellent speech and received a doctor of laws degree. Bachelor's degrees were awarded to fifty-two men and women, the smallest class by far in my administration.

Five of the most senior alumni of the College were in attendance. Oldest of the group and oldest of all living graduates was Raymond Wood '89, who drove down alone from his home in Minneapolis. Next was Dr. Willard Garratt '95, emeritus professor of mathematics at Baker University, Baldwin, Kansas. Then came two members of the Class of 1896, Colonel Edward Clifford, former assistant secretary of the treasury from Washington, D.C., and Dr. George Baxter, trustee and former chairman of the board, from Glendora, California. Youngest of the oldsters was Harry J. Dunbaugh '99, Chicago, another trustee and past chairman of the board.

New at this Commencement but used always thereafter was a replica of the Seal of the College, about five feet in diameter, the result of the labors of Professor George Horton and Mrs. Caine.

I began a trivial personal tradition to which I adhered through all the commencements of my administration. Years before in Minnesota, I had been struck by the fact that President Laurence M. Gould of Carleton College, a good friend, always wore red ties. They were a kind of trademark. I had no idea of doing something like that, but I did think it appropriate to wear a tie of Illinois College colors on state occasions. I bought a blue one for the 1956 commencement. Mrs. Walter Bellatti, wife of the veteran trustee, mentioned at the Commencement reception that my tie was Yale blue—just the thing to wear. As a result, I wore it at all the official occasions. The tie was of moderate width and, while sometimes a

The Administration Takes Shape

little too narrow or a little too wide, it was close enough to the current style to be respectable at all times.

That spring I set a personal record by attending ten commencements and participating in seven of them. Part of the reason was that all three sons had graduation exercises. Stanley, the youngest, graduated with honors from Jacksonville High School, where I gave the invocation. Alan received his bachelor's degree with honors at Macalester College and Clifford, the oldest, received his law degree from the University of Minnesota. Then I presided at the Illinois College Commencement, attended the exercises at MacMurray, and gave five high-school commencement addresses. After marching to Elgar's "Pomp and Circumstance" six times in a little over two weeks, I began to hear it in my sleep.

I enjoyed giving commencement addresses and had the opportunity to experience that happy privilege scores of times in six states. Most of the addresses were delivered at high schools but others were given at nursing schools and at colleges. Some were especially memorable. I found it at first disconcerting when I gave one at the Jacksonville School for the Deaf: all eyes were not on me but on the interpreter who was signing the message twenty feet away. Watching the students at their commencement at the School for the Blind in Jacksonville made it a bit difficult to talk. Delivering the commencement address at Springfield High School, with Governor Stratton sitting on the platform so that he might give out the diplomas to a class that included his daughter, was a special occasion.

Unique among all these commencements was one held about 1943, which I am sure was a national record-breaker. It was conducted in North Dakota at a tiny high school having its final commencement before consolidation. Although there were only four prospective graduates, the superintendent asked me to make it especially good since it was to be the last ever. I promised to do my best.

Two weeks before the occasion, I received a frantic call

from the school superintendent: a crisis had developed. The only minister living in the little town could not deliver the invocation. Nobody in town could or would give the invocation. Would I, for an extra five dollars, do that also? I said that I was on speaking terms with the Lord and that I would be happy to invoke His presence at no additional charge.

As I drove out through the miles of wheat fields on a perfectly gorgeous evening, all seemed right with the world; however, as I neared the two-story wooden building, I sensed trouble. The superintendent and president of the board were in earnest conversation at the entrance. The problem was whether or not to have commencement. I learned that the senior class had shrunk from four members to one. One family had moved away some months before. The sole girl in the class had eloped, and one boy, in a fit of patriotic zeal occasioned by the war, had gone off to join the navy. Only Oscar was left, and he was so bashful that it was doubtful he would show up to be the center of attraction. To have or not to have a commencement exercise without a senior, that was the question.

A capacity crowd was on hand and the speaker had arrived, so it was decided that the show must go on. Someone remembered that Oscar's family was always late for everything, so they planned to wait until 8:15 before starting without him. A few minutes later, a plume of dust was seen down the road, and the car turned out to be the right one. Oscar, red-necked and looking very much out of place in his new suit, got out of the car. The worn-out piano thumped out "Land of Hope and Glory; Land of the Free." We marched in and took our places on the platform, and I gave the invocation, previously appraised at $5.00. When the exercises were over, I had set a new national record of speaking to the smallest graduating class in the country.

The mandate for the early years of the Caine administration was change. If the College were to be true to its history

The Administration Takes Shape

and to its mission, new strategies would have to be devised. One of the changes that occured in the fall of 1958 was the appointment of a new academic dean. The incumbent, Dr. Ernest J. Hildner, Jr., had come to Illinois College in 1939 as dean of the faculty and professor of history. He was a superior teacher, was wholly committed to the College, and was a pillar of the community and a national figure in the Congregational Church. We did not see eye to eye about some of the changes that were necessary for the good of the College. After a number of discussions, he decided that the interests of the College would best be served if he relinquished the deanship and went back to full-time teaching. He did it without rancor and, I think, with some satisfaction.

Dr. Hildner continued to be a pillar of the College. A few years later, when Dr. Smith retired, Dr. Hildner became chairman of the History Department. He and his wife Jean continued to entertain students, to attend every College function, and to serve the College with distinction. As chairman of the Faculty Committee on Athletics, he continued to fill a role he had played as dean, that of seeing to it that athletics, though encouraged, was always subordinate to academics. He retired in 1972 after thity-three years of devoted service to the College and will be remembered as one of the great figures in the long history of the institution.

The new dean, Iver Yeager, was a graduate of Macalester College with a doctorate in theology from the University of Chicago, had served in the navy, and had taught at Missouri Valley and Wooster Colleges. He was a fortunate choice.

Another change took place, this time in the Baxter Hall dining room. At the time, like nearly all of the smaller colleges nationwide, a woman was employed to run the dining facilities. This was no small job: purchasing, cooking, and serving food, and employing and supervising help—both students and outsiders.

However, the time honored system also had some built in inefficiencies. In order to obtain a good price for groceries,

rather large quantities had to be purchased at one time. The storeroom was full of canned goods, and thus a considerable amount of money was tied up. A substantial part of the work of the Business Office consisted of verifying purchases and paying for merchandise, keeping the payrolls, and doing all the other bookkeeping. An even greater problem was that of finding a person who had all the varied skills associated with purchasing, preparing, and serving food as well as managing the people working there, and satisfying those to whom the food was served.

Appearing on the scene were commercial food services that contracted with a college to take over the entire operation at an annual per-student rate. Illinois College then would no longer buy food or figure payrolls. The Business Office had only to write a few checks each year, thereby reducing its workload by more than one-third. Also, complaints about food, if any, were directed at the service and not at the College. These services were found to work so much more efficiently and saved so much by mass-buying that they could make a good profit and still produce better meals at a lower cost than could the College.

Mrs. Mary Munk, who was in charge of Baxter Hall, was a good manager and well regarded. She gave notice that she planned to retire, and I suggested that we look into the possibility of employing a food service in place of getting a new manager. The trustees instructed me to make inquiries and to present a proposition to them for consideration.

Only a very few colleges in Illinois (none downstate) had gone over to food services. Several national groups were looking for clients, but most of them did not want to take on so small an operation. The best of two or three propositions came from Slater Food Service, a Philadelphia organization. My recommendation that they be offered a one-year contract was approved by the trustees. They were generally satisfactory and served the College for the remainder of my administration. Later on, we had them manage our snack bar also.

The Administration Takes Shape

Our experience in "farming out" food services convinced me that it was to the advantage of a small college to employ expert outside agencies to carry on other related activities of a business nature. When the computer arrived, we arranged with a local bank to do our payrolls, including deductions and reports. Illinois College was one of the first in the state to turn over the billing and collection of student loans from the federal government to a Chicago bank that specialized in that work. The result was that the default rate was negligible. In due time, the board adopted a plan to permit its investment agency, Harris Trust, to manage a large part of its endowment under certain regulations. Formerly, every transaction had to be authorized by the Finance Committee.

Another important step was the revision of the process of alumni giving. I had previously developed modern alumni funds at two other colleges and had found the situation at Illinois College out of date. There was no systematic ongoing plan for alumni solicitation. Every alumnus was supposed to pay annual dues to defray the cost of the association and to subscribe to the *Alumni Quarterly*. Only a few alumni paid their dues, and a small minority sent in their subscription money. To have a good alumni organization, it is necessary for everyone to receive the alumni publication, and to become members of the alumni association automatically, rather than by payment of dues. Accordingly, dues and subscriptions were abolished, and every alumnus is now expected to make a contribution to the College. Not long after, we introduced the class agent system, and giving increased from 8.6 percent to 15.7 percent in one year.

In the fall of 1958, enrollment passed the 450 mark, the figure I had told the board must be reached for a successful operation. The women students nearly filled Ellis Hall. Gardner Hall overflowed, and some of the men began to live in Crampton Hall again.

With the buildings now restored, the campus was a place of great beauty, owing in no small degree to the wonderful

trees and shrubs that graced it. The tasteful arrangement and selection of those of more recent origin were due to a remarkable woman to whom the College owes a great debt. Courtney Crouch Wright '12, landscape gardener, had been the unpaid and unofficial landscape planner since about 1930. When the College had no money for nursery stock, she would ask grove owners to donate trees and other plantings or she would raise money herself to pay for them.

Mrs. Wright was elated when we were able to budget some money for new plantings. She told me that while my predecessors had always wanted the campus to look nice, they never had any money to buy what was necessary to keep it so. She supervised the maintenance people in their trimming of trees and setting out new plantings. Probably no person in the history of the College is more responsible for the beauty of the campus, except perhaps Jonathan Baldwin Turner.

Mrs. Wright's knowledge was particularly important when, in the 1960s, calamity befell Jacksonville in the form of the Dutch elm disease. Starting many years before, it ravaged New England and moved relentlessly westward, destroying the elms along the way. Jacksonville, "The Elm City," was properly named; noble elms made a green canopy over the streets. All sorts of methods were tried to stem the disease. One was to gird the trees with a sticky substance calculated to stop the bark beetles from climbing up. Another was to spray with DDT, which killed many birds, including all the robins. Nothing worked. On the campus, scores and scores of trees, some nearly one-hundred years old, died. Cutting them down and rooting out their great stumps, three to five feet in diameter, cost a large amount of money. In the end, hardly an elm remained.

Fortunately, many varieties of trees had been planted so the campus still had a sylvan look, but hundreds of new plantings were required; the selection and placement were decided upon by Mrs. Wright. Because the elms died gradually, our reforestation went on for several years.

The Administration Takes Shape

The College expressed its pride in the fact that one of its seniors, Carole Ann McNamara '59, was awarded a Fulbright fellowship for study in France; a few years later she became a valued member of the faculty.

The National Science Foundation announced that Illinois College had one of the highest percentages of graduates receiving doctorates in the field of science of any educational institution in the nation. Over a ten year period, fifty-six alumni had earned that distinction.

Two distinguished visitors that year were especially interesting. One, Senator Paul Douglas of Illinois, celebrated his birthday with a cake at our home. He was a long-time friend of Dr. and Mrs. Joe Patterson Smith from their days at the University of Chicago. The second was Charles Bryan, vice president of the Pullman Company, who accepted the invitation to come because he was a relative of the College's most distinguished graduate, William Jennings Bryan.

One of the fine gifts to the College that year, which was given with the proviso that the donor not be revealed at that time, was an electronic Wurlitzer organ for the chapel in Jones Hall. Later transferred to Rammelkamp Chapel, it was the gift of Arthur and Charlotte Hart, Classes of '25 and '26. He was later elected a trustee and was one of the most generous for years to come. This organ replaced the regular pipe organ that had been installed in the Jacksonville Female Academy and subsequently transferred to the College when the academy went out of business in 1904. It had wheezed its last and could not be repaired.

After World War II, the GI Bill became the major source of aid for students all over the nation. This great infusion of financial assistance relieved institutions of higher learning of a considerable part of the burden of assisting needy students to go to college. By 1958, the number of prospective students qualifying for such assistance had greatly diminished. With the Cold War heating up, Congress authorized the National Defense Student Loan Program (NDSL) to assure continuing

high enrollments at colleges lest the Soviet Union outstrip the United States in technical developments.

Few realized that this was a case of history repeating itself: colleges were again benefiting from a military threat. One of the reasons that Illinois College's Jonathan Baldwin Turner, "Father of the Land-Grant Colleges," was able to get his idea of an agricultural and manual arts institution established with money from the federal government was that each of them was required to have a Reserve Officers Training Corps (ROTC). This legislation was enacted and signed by President Lincoln, in part because the Civil War was being fought and the need for army officers was acute. Now, the threat from the Soviet Union seemed to justify aid to students so that the United States might not fall behind in the arms race.

Like nearly every governmental assistance program, the NDSL grew to enormous size as time went on. When it became inappropriate to use the word *Defense* in the title, the word was changed to *Direct*.

Illinois College received its initial allotment of NDSL money in time to use it during the second semester of the 1958–1959 year. The first allocation, in the amount of $5,161, was for freshmen only. Applications totaled $9,810. Each college was required to supply 10 percent of the loan fund from its own resources. Students were not required to pay interest or to begin repayments while enrolled in college, and repayments became a part of a revolving fund for lending to later students. The NDSL was a great help to the colleges because students could borrow money that might otherwise have been supplied as direct aid from the colleges. This modest loan program for students from very low income families was made more liberal as time went on and came to take the form of outright grants as well as loans.

In the fall of 1958, the state of Illinois began to make tuition grants to entering freshmen. Illinois College was allocated the modest sum of $5,250, which went to ten freshmen on the basis of financial need and academic ability.

The Administration Takes Shape

Politicians can never resist the voter appeal of greater financial assistance for every sort of new program, so the stringent requirements were gradually relaxed and the amount of money rapidly increased. In time, any student admitted was eligible, and the family income threshold was raised so that most students were receiving direct aid.

Few persons are fully aware of the effects of the vast amounts of money from tax sources, both state and federal, granted to college students beginning with the GI Bill. Before World War II, a low percentage of young people attended college. Ambitious students from families with few financial resources had a real struggle to obtain higher education. Like thousands of others, I was a case in point.

After graduating as valedictorian in a class of seven at age sixteen, I had to work for two years to obtain money for college. By working on a farm, selling magazine subscriptions, and clerking in a general store, I saved up $600 and acquired some clothes. I attended college on a tuition scholarship and worked in a grocery store twenty-five hours a week during the college season. During my three undergraduate summers, I worked as a farm laborer, as a member of a surveying crew, and as a book salesman. At graduation, I owed a relative $400. It was a tough grind, but I would not have missed it for anything. I got a teaching job paying $1440 per year and paid off my debt in the first year.

My experience was typical. Generations of Illinois College men fired furnaces, worked in restaurants, put on screens and storm windows, and did all sorts of work in the summers that, along with generous grants from the College, enabled them to get an education. More often, the needy women students lived with families, receiving room and board in exchange for their domestic labor. The proudest boasts of many students, and among their fondest memories as undergraduates, are of their struggles to get an education.

I witnessed the total transformation from a high degree of self-reliance among families to substantial dependency on

government aid. This was paralleled by what went on in society in general, and the results, while defensible, are not all positive. I have been shocked in my later years by the strange assertion that support in and out of college is the right of all, whether or not they put forth their best efforts. I believe that a great part of the financial problems and some of the national moral dilemmas are the results of the decline in self-reliance promoted by well-meaning but misguided people whose ideas became government policy.

When parents and students complained about the high cost of attending college, they were surprised when told that it was easier to finance a college education in the 1970s than ever before. I was a consultant, after my retirement, for a small college in Tennessee where hardly a single student paid any appreciable amount of money to attend. Most students were totally supported—board, room, tuition, clothes, transportation, and incidentals—from tax funds. Today, the majority of the student population is at least partly supported by state or federal grants and loans. Even at private colleges, including some that refuse to take tax money for any direct purpose, many of their students are supported, in part, by tax money.

Although the number of students of limited means has increased since the 1950s, the number wanting to work has declined. At the better colleges this is attributable, in part, to the greater demands imposed by the institution on the time of the students; among many students, however, it also reflects the completely human tendency to take what one can get with the least effort. When economies are contemplated in state and federal budgets, defense and student aid are two of the relatively untouchable items. I believe that some decrease in that easy money would do little harm to enrollments and might do something for character building. A little more personal responsibility and a reduction in dependency on government would not be a bad thing for society.

Aside from making it much easier to go to college, the

assistance has made it much easier for colleges to finance their operations. The colleges with the least money used to be the ones that had to find the largest proportion of assistance for their students. What used to be the hardest bills to collect are now paid by the government.

In those days of less affluence and greater effort and individual sacrifice, collective kindness was not absent. One such incident at Illinois College in 1958 was both touching and inspiring. An Oriental family, who had come to the United States and settled in California after World War II, had a boy enrolled at Illinois College. He did not have the money to go home for Christmas, and his family could not supply it. What happened was revealed in a letter I received later from his father, which said, in part: "Boys and girls in the dormitories collected money and bought a round trip ticket from St. Louis to San Francisco and gave it to my son as a Christmas present. So he came home when our Christmas program was going on. We find another example of Christian love living and working in this country."

A special educational feature of the year at the College came as the result of a Ford Foundation gift. Encyclopaedia Britannica, under a grant from the Fund for the Advancement of Education, had begun an experiment in teaching by films. The world renowned British historian, Arnold Toynbee, filmed a series of lectures, "A Changing World in the Light of History." This series was made into an evening course and some twenty-five townspeople along with students signed up for it. Although the series was good, it again disproved the theory that a great master on film is better than a live teacher of lesser fame.

3
The 1960s Begin:
1960–1962

The normal work load of a college president is very heavy, but it was even more so in the early days of my administration. In the early 1960s, the College was planning and constructing buildings with no one on the staff who could be of much help in work of that kind. I was also the only staff person involved in fund raising, and much more than the normal number of faculty members were being added, both as replacements and for newly created positions.

The steady and substantial growth of the student body is indicated by the changing housing arrangements. In the middle 1950s, Crampton Hall had ample room for all the women who needed campus living quarters, and newly erected Gardner Hall was only partly occupied by all the men residing on campus. When Ellis Hall was occupied by the women in the fall of 1957, Crampton was emptied but the new facility was not filled. Not long after, Gardner overflowed and some of the men moved back into Crampton. By 1960, more rooms were needed for both men and women. Colonial Inn on State Street, which had been a private hotel, had been used as the dormitory for students of nursing at Passavant Hospital. It became the second women's dormitory. In addition to filling Gardner and Crampton, men took up residence in Fayerweather House. In 1962, the capacity of Ellis was doubled, but in another year more rooms were needed for both men and women.

With increased enrollment came the need for more faculty.

The 1960s Begin

This need coincided with an acute shortage of qualified college professors, and many substandard and poorly prepared candidates had no trouble finding jobs. The only advantage to the situation was that it was easy to dismiss an unsatisfactory teacher because he or she could easily find another position. Many transient instructors graced the faculty rolls during these years.

Two good permanent appointments—faculty members who continued to serve for years beyond my tenure—were made in this period. One new faculty member, Dr. Wilbur Chien, was born in China but had graduate degrees from American institutions. Another real find was Don Filson, the son of friends. His mother was a national leader in the Presbyterian Church, and his father was a distinguished biblical scholar and teacher and later dean of McCormick Theological Seminary. As head of the Chemistry Department, Don brought stability to a segment of the College in deep trouble; he turned out to be one of the most valuable members of the faculty.

The worst year from the standpoint of faculty recruitment was probably 1961–1962, when two faculty members died, one suffered a disabling mental breakdown, three resigned to go back to graduate school, and one moved on to another college. Several new positions also had to be filled. From the great departure at the end of the Selden administration to the middle of the 1960s, the faculty was in flux. Getting proper persons for faculty and staff positions was a major problem.

While the faculty at the time of my retirement was a very good one, I doubt that it was any better than the one I inherited. The faculty of the mid-1950s had a high percentage of excellent teachers, and it was not until many years later that faculty quality again measured up to the earlier times. I am sure that at no time in the history of the College was turnover as rapid as in the first half of my presidency, just as there had never been a time when so many new positions had been created. In the later days of my term in office, the major

problem was not to find good scholars but to persuade professors that doing an adequate job extended far beyond teaching classes effectively. The care and concern of faculty members for students and their willingness to participate in general college life were characteristics that made the faculty in earlier days so effective. It is fitting that so many of the old timers, now gone, are remembered by memorials raised to them by grateful men and women who were their students.

With the new decade, the ultimate authority at the College shifted to new hands. Only seven of the trustees I first encountered remained on the board. F. Osborne Elliott succeeded his father who had served for forty-one years. Dr. Garm Norbury, longtime secretary of the trustees, had asked Dr. Robert Hartman '35, to help him with that work. Dr. Hartman succeeded him as secretary. Arthur Hart, later to be vice chairman and one of the most generous and able members of the board, was elected in 1960.

Almost unknowingly, colleges and universities, especially those of the private sector, were making decisions that could mean life or death. It was the time of unprecedented enrollment increases, and the money to build was easy to obtain. More construction of educational and auxiliary buildings was taking place than at any time before and probably ever again. Far too many people in positions of educational authority assumed that growth was to be a continuous process—an extrapolation of what was going on. Like the investors before the stock market crash of 1929, little thought was given to the fact that boom times are seldom more than a temporary phenomenon.

These educational leaders failed to assess three factors that were the causes of the rapid expansion but would not persist. The first was a bulge in the number of young people of college age. As a result of the total mobilization for war in the early 1940s, marriages were delayed until the men came home. This abnormal marriage rate, lasting but a short time, resulted in a baby boom of unprecedented proportions. In the

The 1960s Begin

early 1960s, those babies were flooding the upper grades of elementary and secondary schools and beginning to spill over into colleges. Already the lower grades were beginning to shrink to normal size, foreshadowing a decline in college-age men and women in another decade.

The second factor was that every state in the union was in the process of greatly expanding its tax-supported higher educational facilities. Before 1960, states like New York, New Jersey, and Massachusetts depended largely on private institutions for higher education. Now these states, along with the others, multiplied the number and capacity of their tax-supported institutions of higher education. Before they did so, many of their students could not find places near home to go to college. Thus, they came west and inundated the Midwest colleges. A few years later, when their own home states had provided facilities, they found no reason to go so far away, and private colleges that had boasted of their national student bodies were forced to gather their enrollments from nearer at hand. Because they had not counted on this decrease in enrollment from distant places, college enrollments never reached optimistically anticipated levels.

Illinois itself is a good example of the expansion and overexpansion of tax-supported higher education. The teachers' colleges at Normal, Macomb, Carbondale, and Charleston became ambitious, full-scale universities hoping to rival the University of Illinois in size and prestige. Then there was the attempt that succeeded in putting every acre of land in the state, except the Jacksonville area and a few other sections scattered north of Chicago, into a junior college district. A new university was opened in Chicago, and, taking advantage of the enthusiasm of the moment, ambitious Springfield boosters succeeded in getting through legislation establishing Sangamon State University, an institution that never achieved either the size or the quality its promoters anticipated. It was not really needed.

The third factor was the increase in the percentage of the

college-age population attending institutions of higher learning. Fueled by generous grants and loan programs from both federal and state governments and often inspired by military draft deferments for men attending college, the percentage of enrollments skyrocketed. The figure had been pushed up from below 20 percent to more than 50 percent, and to expect further increases was unrealistic. This percentage increase was more the cause of swelling enrollments than even the population increase.

What defies explanation, in retrospect, is why the private sector did not take into account the special factors that produced these temporary boom times. Students do not enter college until they have lived some eighteen years, and first-grade enrollments are an indicator of the size of freshman college classes a dozen years later. Long before students knock on the doors of colleges, their numbers are known.

This exuberant desire to build educational facilities beyond needs took place at all levels. Jacksonville completed two new public-school buildings just about the time enrollment began to decline. Before the 1970s ended, one grade school was closed and it was acknowledged that only one of two junior high schools was required. Hundreds of private colleges were crippled by the poor judgment that produced unneeded educational and dormitory space, often built with borrowed money. One good Midwest college with a normal enrollment of about 800 built for 1600, managed at the high point to enroll about 1200, and then declined to less than 700; it was saddled with crippling debts on its unnecessary and unused facilities. State institutions followed the same pattern. The two nearest Jacksonville, Lincoln Land Community College and Sangamon State University, never approached their projected sizes.

One of the wisest decisions ever made by the trustees of Illinois College was to expand its capacity to only 800 students, to build only as pressure dictated, and to pay for all nonrevenue producing buildings as they were built. To that

decision as much as to any other can be attributed the fact that Illinois College in the 1980s is so much better off than most of its sister institutions.

The colleges had some excuses beyond their own judgments for following the primrose path. The federal government lured them into unwise construction by partial grants and low-interest loans. Even the enormous Ford Foundation, the most generous to education of all the foundations, preached and practiced a policy that caused serious losses to the endowment of many colleges and reduced its own assets by one-third. The foundation proposed that colleges invest a part of their endowments in growth stocks rather than looking for those with high yields. To compensate for the lower returns on the growth stocks, the colleges would sell off some of the appreciation to make up for the loss in earnings. There was only one problem with this novel scheme. It assumed that growth stocks would always grow—that is, increase in value.

The time came when stocks no longer increased in value. That meant that to sell stocks to maintain current income was actually dipping into endowment to support current operations. This was often done under the charade of temporary borrowing. During my days of consulting with endangered colleges after my retirement, I came across two colleges with fair endowments shown on the books but all of which had been borrowed piecemeal for current operations. In other words, their endowments were gone.

An additional reason why many colleges went astray in the boom times was that many of the new presidents, having never experienced depression or hard times, did not have the memory nor were they aware of the possibility that what went up might come down.

One of the most significant new developments for the financial support of the private sector of higher education took place in the 1950s: financial assistance from business and industry of a cooperative and sustained scale. It began

when the presidents of Earlham and Wabash Colleges in Indiana decided that they could get better support from certain corporations in their territory if they went together to make the requests. They found that industrial leaders welcomed this approach. While industries had desired to support private education, they often had difficulty in choosing between colleges and, thus, they refrained from giving. A united fund approach would be welcomed.

These two men interested the president of United States Steel in sponsoring a meeting of a few representatives from several states to talk over the idea. With the costs underwritten by the company, certain representative institutions were asked to send a person to the conference. I became the Minnesota representative to the meeting in Cincinnati. This conference sparked the formation of state associations of private colleges over the whole nation. One of the first was the Minnesota group, organized in 1952. I was the secretary and served with two others as the committee that organized the business solicitation for the first year or two, until a full-time executive was employed. In Illinois, a similar association was organized a year or so later.

There is an interesting personal footnote to the organization of state associations. As an insider, I learned that U.S. Steel was going to make a gift to every state association, to help persuade other businesses to respond to the new plan. Only states having organizations at the time of the gift would share in the distribution. I had recently come to Minnesota from North Dakota, where there was only a single private college. I gave the information to that institution, Jamestown College, and told them they had better quickly organize a North Dakota association. They did, using local members of their board as officers. They received a portion of the money.

In Minnesota, every private college—not a large number—was a member of the association. It was an ideal state for such an organization. All of the colleges were of a similar moderate size, and there were no great private universities.

The 1960s Begin

When I came to Illinois, I discovered a much different situation. In Illinois, it was not advisable for Northwestern, DePaul, Chicago, and the other large private universities to join in the enterprise. It turned out that the association's efforts were in competition with the giants of private education. While the Illinois association never was as effective as the one in Minnesota, it was still a great help.

In 1960, a national effort of the same type was launched. The state associations discovered that certain large interstate corporations were not happy to be solicited in many different states. They would prefer to give to the private college movement in one lump sum. This resulted in the formation of the Independent College Fund of America with funds given to it distributed according to an agreed-upon formula among the state associations. It so happened that I was one of the two college presidents from Illinois to go to New York to take part in the solicitation that established support for that organization. It was an exciting experience. I recall going to ITT and being told of their loss of millions of dollars in assets because Castro had just confiscated all their property in Cuba.

To have had a part in the creation of this landmark movement to get substantial support from industry for private higher education has been a source of great satisfaction to me. In the initial solicitations, a major question was always whether or not corporate executives could legally give away "stockholders' money." A Supreme Court decision ruled that they could. One of the major benefits to college presidents who did the solicitation was the opportunity to get to know the problems of industry and to make common cause for private enterprise. During the course of visits to corporations, I had the privilege, especially in the early days of the movement, to talk with the major leaders of industry and business on numerous occasions.

The Jacksonville community developed a variation of the movement for the joint support of colleges by business. The

presidents of Illinois College and MacMurray had trouble getting local support from business institutions on the basis of service to the community. Businessmen felt that if they gave to one, they would have to give to the other. The obvious answer seemed to be to organize a joint solicitation with the proceeds to be divided between the two colleges. We presidents arranged for an organization to make such a Jacksonville solicitation. Dr. Robert Hartman, one of the members of the original committee, proposed to call it by the catchy acronymn CACHE, the Committee for the Advancement of Community Higher Education. Since then, there has been an annual canvass. The amount subscribed, while important, is far below that raised by similar communities with a single college.

It would be easy to write a book about incidents connected with my fund raising at three colleges and for state associations. I am unable to resist including a couple of examples from the two colleges I served early in my career. A well-to-do farmer from the Red River valley had twin daughters who were freshmen at Jamestown College shortly after World War II. I had been a friend of the family for some time. During the Thanksgiving recess, the mother and the twins were caught in a blinding snowstorm on their way to Fargo. All three were killed at a railroad crossing. The father asked me to speak at the funeral and later invited me to an auction sale of some of his fine cattle. The second invitation, which came months later, surprised me, but I went. At the sale, he gave me one of his prize cows for the College; we sold it with the others.

Sometimes a money raising effort fails but still is interesting. Such was the case at Macalester College not long before I came to Jacksonville. I drove into the far North Woods of Minnesota on the trail of an old man who lived with his wife in as small a town as one can imagine. They had no children but had become very rich when iron ore was discovered on their farm years before.

The 1960s Begin

After a late morning conversation and lunch, the man asked me to take a ride with him so that he could show me the town. There was little to see. It was located along a road in the woods with a few places of business on each side of the street for only a couple of blocks. Then he turned off on a side road and we came to an overgrown little cemetery, so neglected that it hardly could be distinguished from the woods around it. In the center was what he really wanted to show me—a good-sized marble mausoleum to hold the bones of himself and his wife. His explanation of why he built the mausoleum was not what one would expect. He said he had had it constructed "to dress up the cemetery." Sad to say, Macalester never received a dime from him, then or later.

Most of my especially interesting encounters with donors at Illinois College will never be recorded, but here is one from those early days. Dr. Egerton Crispin '02 had been a highly successful physician who with his wife retired in the Los Angeles area. A man of considerable means, his name came up as a prime prospect for a major gift in our first financial campaign which was to secure the funds for the chapel and the science hall. Correspondence with Dr. Crispin revealed that he was willing to discuss a major contribution.

Whenever I went to California on College business, I would stay at the home of Dr. and Mrs. George Baxter. Dr. Baxter was an old friend of Dr. Crispin. Dr. Baxter, on this trip, drove me over to the Crispin home. After tea and conversation, Dr. Baxter and Mrs. Crispin withdrew so that I could talk to Dr. Crispin privately. I sensed immediately that something was wrong.

He said he could not give any money to the College; it was not that he did not want to but that he could not. I had great difficulty accepting that answer because I knew he was a wealthy man and because his letters gave every indication that he was going to make a gift. So agitated was he that he became incoherent, and I thought he was going to have a

heart attack. His wife came in and Dr. Baxter and I made as graceful an exit as the situation allowed.

On the way back, we stopped at Dr. Baxter's club, and I wrote a note to Mrs. Crispin saying that I was unaware that her husband had aged so much and I was sorry to have upset him so. Utterly discouraged, I returned to Jacksonville only to learn that a message arrived from Dr. Baxter requesting that I telephone him immediately.

He had been in touch with Mrs. Crispin and had discovered that, the day before I saw them, the court as a result of some litigation involving Dr. Crispin had declared him to be incompetent as a result of his age. It was true that now he could not give anyone any money, much as he wanted to help the College. However, all his assets were to go to Mrs. Crispin, and she had considerable holdings in her own name. She had already mailed some stocks to me as his gift to help construct the science hall. The value of the stocks was $172,000. We named the building Crispin Science Hall.

Modern-day fund raising is very different from that of pre–World War II days, which illustrates just how much the job of a college president has changed. On the financial side, there were no general solicitations nor many programs for raising money from alumni. Businesses did not contribute as they do now. A few large donors like the Rockefellers gave millions, and some very wealthy persons gave to many colleges related to their church. Getting funds now is on the retail scale rather than the wholesale, as it once was.

Travel itself was different. It took days to get to New York, and my predecessors would go for some meetings and a week of seeing wealthy potential donors a couple of times a year. Presidents were a somewhat different breed also. Most church-related colleges had clergymen for their chief administrative officers. Presidents also were generally more scholarly. Today, private colleges look for men or women of business ability who know public relations and fund raising. There are few ministers among them. I recall hearing how,

The 1960s Begin

when Commencement was over, President Rammelkamp would leave for his cottage in Michigan for the summer. Today, taking a summer off is impossible. One is lucky to get a month off and often that is in fragments.

It was in the turbulent era just after World War II that the old style president proved ineffective and a new breed arose. Many church-related colleges that had never had other than a minister for a president have not had one since. Illinois College has been the exception in that most of its presidents have been laymen.

As a Presbyterian, I was active in church councils in the promotion of the church colleges. I headed a movement that caused the annual Synod meetings to be held in rotation on the church-related campuses. I was elected chairman of the General Council of the Synod of Illinois, the only layman ever to hold that position. The General Council was in effect the executive committee of the Synod and acted for that body when it was not in session. On the national scene, I was a member of the committee that developed the Presbyterian College Scholarship program.

In 1960, the Kiwanis Club sponsored a unique event at the College gymnasium. It was a banquet for all the football squads of the city—Jacksonville High School, Routt, the School for the Deaf, and Illinois College. The main speaker was Ray Eliot (formerly Ray Nuspickel), head coach at the University of Illinois where he had gone from the same position at Illinois College.

For those who might not remember, television has not been here forever. And in 1960 there were no television sets on the campus. Mrs. Frank F. Byrom, a relative of Mrs. Louise Becker, the housemother who served so well for years, on a visit here decided that there should be television sets in the lounge of every dormitory, so she bought them.

One of the chief concerns of the College was the inadequate compensation of faculty members. The first faculty salary schedule was adopted in 1956, along with guidelines

for promotion and tenure. Two years later, this schedule was obsolete and a new one adopted. In 1960, a third schedule was implemented with the salaries of professors increased $2,000 over those of 1956. At a time when inflation was not a consideration, this represented a great gain for all members of the faculty.

Now that the professors were more adequately compensated, better fringe benefits became an important consideration. At that time, the benefits consisted of a retirement fund supported by a contribution of 5 percent of salary from the faculty member and a matching amount from the College. There was also a very small life insurance policy. The faculty talked over all possible fringe benefits and finally agreed on the order in which they would like them introduced. The greatest desire of the higher-ranking members particularly was a system of sabbatical leaves. A plan was drawn up whereby full and associate professors would be eligible for a one-semester leave with pay if they had been on the faculty at least six years and were not within five years of retirement. The number of leaves, if any, would depend upon what the College could afford. The board adopted the plan, and Dr. Hildner was granted the first sabbatical. He spent it in Spain doing research where he had studied more than thirty years before in preparation for his doctorate. Dr. Malcolm F. Stewart received the sabbatical the next year. He went to Thailand and India to brush up on Eastern philosophy and religion.

Later on, two or three faculty members would receive sabbaticals in a single year. If they desired and if it could be arranged, some would take a full-year sabbatical at half pay rather than a semester at full pay. In some cases, further adjustments were made. For example, Dr. Seybold was unable to take a semester off because her aged mother lived with her. She could get away in the summer because her sister could come and stay with their mother. The committee allowed her a modest sum to enable her to live and study in England one summer. During a sabbatical, the professor

could not be gainfully employed. The value of the experience to the College was a major factor in awarding the leave.

Two members of the faculty who stayed on beyond my retirement began their work at Illinois College that year—Donald Eldred, Dean of Students, and Geraldine Staley, who came to teach speech and handle debate and who later switched to her first love, dramatics.

The relentless march of years brought more changes to the trustees. Harry Dunbaugh found it necessary to retire after twenty-six years as a member of the board, seventeen as chairman. He had joined the Chicago law firm of Ishem, Lincoln, and Beil when Robert Lincoln was an active member. Forest Siefkin '12, vice president of International Harvester, also joined the ranks of the emeriti.

While the several trustees who served for short periods are not included in this narrative, those who joined the board and remained as long as I did are all mentioned. One who came on and retired before I did deserves to be named because of his unique contribution to the College. He was David Milligan of Des Moines, Iowa, a layman whose great services to the Congregational Churches caused Chairman Hoskins to nominate him. He owned a chain of grain elevators in Iowa and was well versed in farm management.

In 1950, Judge William Gardner '84 had left his farm holdings in southwest Iowa to the College. It was difficult for the College to oversee the management of the farms at such a distance. By the late 1950s, the board decided to dispose of this property, much of which was rough land in need of considerable work to make it more productive. By trades, sales, and resales over a dozen years, all the property was disposed of. Mr. Milligan was advisor to all the transactions and took the initiative in the negotiations at no cost to the College.

Harry Dunbaugh's interest in the College did not end with his retirement from the board. I had a standing invitation to stay with the Dunbaughs whenever I was in Chicago. He and Mrs. Dunbaugh were ideal hosts, and they called one of the

Harry J. Dunbaugh '99, trustee and chairman of the board, and major benefactor of Illinois College, is honored at the 1961 Commencement.

rooms in their Hubbard Woods house mine. He went to his office every day, but as the infirmities of age crept up on him, he had to modify his life style. We at first took the train into the city and walked the half mile to his office. Later, he had to shorten his days and still later had to be driven to his office. Finally, he could make the trip no more. But as long as I was President, I stayed at their home when I went to Chicago.

One day in 1964, when we arrived at his office building after our walk from the depot, he asked me to come up to his office rather than to go on about my work. When we were seated he began with a bit of history. He said that back around 1920 the Alumni Association of Illinois College had decided to stage a campaign to get members to include the

The 1960s Begin

College in their wills. Harry, William Jennings Bryan, and another man whose name was unfamiliar to me were appointed to head the effort. He said that both of the other men had died without leaving a penny to the College. That would not be so with him. His next words burned themselves into my memory so that I can quote them. "I'm going to leave you (meaning the College) a million dollars." I was stunned.

Harry went on to say that it would be a long time before the College would get the money because it would not go to the College until the death of his wife (who was younger than he). He was setting up a trust of $1,000,000 with the income to go to Mrs. Dunbaugh as long as she lived and then to the College for general endowment. When he died in the winter of 1968, we received legal confirmation of the gift. Although I did not know it then, it was the second million-dollar bequest reported to me. The Pixley bequest exceeded that eventually but largely because of appreciation between the earlier date when it was written and its maturity. How much the Dunbaugh trust has appreciated is unknown to me.

In 1961, two new trustees of special merit were elected. One was Lyndle Hess '30, vice president of Libby, McNeill, and Libby, later to be their president and then chairman of the board. The other was Walter E. Thwaite, field representative of Research Corporation, whose business it was to make research grants to students at colleges and universities in the Midwest. While he served only briefly before he was killed in an automobile accident, he did some special things for the College. When he saw something he did not believe was just right in a building, he would correct it. He did not fancy the many rather conspicuous electrical outlets on the front of the stage in the chapel, so he bought new ones. He thought the pulpit and lectern would look better if they had antependia, so he provided them. When it came time to dedicate the new Crispin Science Hall, which was to be done at Commencement, he said he would get the speaker for the dedication and for Commencement at his own expense. For

the dedication, he invited a noted scientist, Dr. Calvin A. VanderWerf, chairman of the chemistry department of the University of Kansas, and for Commencement, the world-renowned physicist, Dr. James Van Allen.

In 1962, what were among the best as well as the longest teaching careers at Illinois College came to an end. Professors Earle B. Miller (mathematics) and Joe Patterson Smith (history) concluded thirty-five years of teaching. Both were slated for retirement, but Professor Miller died unexpectedly in March. Dr. Miller was a master teacher and the author of two widely used college mathematics textbooks. His grateful students established a series of mathematics prizes in his memory. Dr. Smith passed away in the same manner less than a year later but after he had retired.

Joe Pat, as Dr. Smith was affectionately known, was a unique and forceful character. Upon graduation from high school he had enlisted in the Marine Corps in 1915 and was

At the 1961 Commencement, Dr. George Baxter '96 was awarded a doctor of humane letters degree. A trustee for thirty-seven years and chairman of the Board of Trustees from 1932 to 1937, he donated the funds for Baxter Hall.

The 1960s Begin

blinded in action. He sought further education and received his doctorate in history from the University of Chicago and spent his entire teaching career at Illinois College, where he was a dominant figure. His talented wife, Alma, was in no small measure responsible for his remarkable career. She was not only his eyes but a moderating influence on his strong opinions.

At his death, former students and friends raised in excess of $15,000 to endow a lectureship in his name. This annual lecture has become one of the important events on the campus and has attracted speakers of national importance. The first was Dr. Douglas Crain of Stanford University. Two of the other early annual lecturers were the Smiths' personal friend, Senator Paul Douglas, and South Dakota's George McGovern, later the Democratic candidate for president of the United States. Both reflected Dr. Smith's philosophy.

Dr. Eleanor Miller, professor of psychology, who along with her husband Earle and Dr. Smith had joined the faculty in 1927, taught for a few more years before reaching retirement age. She was a great teacher and a constructive force in the community as well as on the campus. These three superb teachers and strong personalities were among those most responsible for the academic strength of Illinois College during their lives.

Other deaths struck the campus. In the spring of 1962, C. B. Wilson, business manager since 1957, died following a long illness. For almost a year, Leah Schramm and I carried on the management of the business affairs because he was unable to function. The next year, Dr. E. Heyse Dummer, professor of German for four years, died suddenly.

In 1963 and 1964, five trustees passed away. Walter Bellatti '05 served on the Board for forty-three years and had been chairman of the Finance Committee since 1930. In his second year as a trustee, Walter Thwaite died in an automobile accident. Dr. Norbury passed away in his thirty-fifth year as a trustee. He had served as secretary of the board since

1946. A leader in the medical profession, he was a past president of the Illinois Medical Association. His classmate Forest Siefkin died a few months later. A trustee for fifteen years, he had a highly successful career with International Harvester, ending as vice president and general counsel. Shortly thereafter, after forty years as a trustee, Carl Robinson '09, once principal of Whipple Academy, a former member of the Illinois General Assembly, a leading attorney, and a Presbyterian church worker, died.

For the fourth time in a decade, an Illinois College senior was awarded a Fulbright fellowship for postgraduate study overseas. William Roosen of the Class of 1962 was the honoree.

A college president can hardly fail to be drawn into many interesting enterprises not specifically related to his or her regular duties. In 1961, I was named by Governor Otto Kerner to a commission to recommend legislation to curb the many diploma mills which operated from addresses in this state. Some were no more than a post office box. They sell certifications or academic degrees at stated prices and require only token efforts on the part of buyers. Strangely enough, some members of the clergy acquire doctorates in this manner. Another large market are those persons in foreign countries who become eligible for positions or promotions in government service if they have been awarded a bachelor's degree, no matter what the source.

No small number of these dubious degrees, such as "doctorate in metaphysics," are used by unscrupulous promoters and writers. Some of the degrees are simply a way of stroking the human ego even when they yield no monetary advantages. In addition, there are certifications of all sorts that make blue-collar workers as well as others seem qualified to do lucrative work. Displaying the certificate indicates to the public that they are qualified artisans.

We had interesting meetings but accomplished little. Many of those who subscribed to these services were fully aware

The 1960s Begin

that they were simply buying the degree or the certification for their own advantage. Those who were victims of actual fraudulent promises could already sue for damages. The problem of enacting legislation to put diploma mills out of business becomes apparent when one considers the matter of curbing the ordination of clergymen who seek to be recognized as ministers for economic advantages. Some legitimate churches require certain academic training for ordination while others do not. Just what a church is cannot be clearly defined. Nonreligious individuals or groups have organized what is called a church to conduct certain financial activities because of tax exemptions.

I also accepted a leadership role in a national project of the Presbyterian Church. Seventy conferences were being held throughout the nation to discuss the nature of the ministry of the church. These conferences were attended by equal numbers of clergy and leading lay persons. I was the leader of several of these held in Illinois and Indiana.

One of the historic special events in 1962 was the celebration of the centennial of the establishment of the land grant colleges, an event in which an Illinois College faculty member had played such an important role. Jonathan Baldwin Turner came to Illinois College in 1833, immediately upon graduation from Yale College. He continued on the faculty here until 1847, when he resigned under pressure after being charged with holding unorthodox religious beliefs.

Turner earned a lasting place in American history for several reasons. Before the invention of barbed wire, no inexpensive and practical way had been devised to keep cattle out of grain fields. Turner solved the problem by bringing in the Osage orange tree, which made a hedge "bull strong and hog tight." Considered a leading horticulturist, he developed species of fruit including raspberries that flourished in the Illinois climate. Most of all, he believed in the full expansion of the public educational system. He was responsible for the founding of Illinois State Normal, now Illinois State Univer-

sity, located in a community named Normal for the institution developed there. His aim was to assure a supply of competent teachers for elementary schools.

Turner also advocated the training of farmers and artisans so that agriculture and industry could flourish. He conceived the idea of having the federal government establish in every state an institution for training in agriculture and mechanical arts.

A friend of Abraham Lincoln, Turner is credited with persuading the president to sign the Morrill Act, which granted each state 30,000 acres of land per each of its members of Congress, to be sold to establish such an institution in each state. One factor in the passage of this measure was the requirement that each of these institutions establish a Reserve Officers Training Corps. Some of the states established separate institutions. Iowa had a land-grant college at Ames. Indiana started Purdue as its agricultural and mechanical arts college. Others, like Minnesota and Illinois, incorporated their entire programs in one institution.

Brought into being by the Morrill Act, the University of Illinois dates its founding to the passage of that act in 1862. Mindful of the fact that Turner of Illinois College was responsible for the founding of the university, the College was included in the celebration of the centennial. Since Yale founded Illinois College and educated Turner as well, it was fitting that the university take note of that fact.

President Kingman Brewster of Yale was the chief speaker at the Centennial Convocation at the University of Illinois, and I brought greetings to the assembly from the university's "parent institution." President David Henry also thought it appropriate to pay his respects to the "parent" by coming to Jacksonville and presenting a plaque acknowledging Turner's accomplishments. We arranged a special convocation.

It was decided that the best location for the bronze marker would be on a stone set in the middle of the campus. The *Jacksonville Journal Courier*, Illinois' oldest newspaper, of-

fered to supply a granite marker from Vermont, Turner's home state. The inscription reads:

This tablet honors the memory of Jonathan Baldwin Turner, Professor of English at Illinois College, Great Citizen of Illinois, who in February, 1852, first publicly proposed Federal Aid for a system of agricultural and industrial universities, and whose devoted efforts toward the realization of this concept earned him the title: "Father of the Land Grant Colleges." Erected April 13, 1962, in the Centennial Year of the University of Illinois.

The impressive exercises were attended by thirty-two of Turner's descendants. Among them was a grandson, the Reverend Dr. C. A. Carriel, a 1906 graduate of Illinois College. Also present was a great-granddaughter, Mrs. Anita Rundquist, who with her husband, John, farmed the old Turner land near Butler; she later became a trustee of the College. The next generation was represented by John Unger, a student at the University of Illinois. The Rundquists later transplanted from the farm an Osage orange shoot to a site near the campus marker. It is now a large tree.

A luncheon for the Turner descendants, President Henry, and other guests was held at our home after the ceremony. Others present included William M. Kuhfuss, president of the Illinois Agricultural Association and later president of the American Farm Bureau; Dr. Clyde Walton, Illinois State Historian; and Dr. Clyde M. Duncan of the University of Missouri, who wrote *Warrior Schoolmaster,* a biography of Turner.

Turner has been well memorialized. On the campus there is the stone, the Osage orange tree, and a dormitory bearing his name. A public junior high school adjacent to the campus is named for him. His name also graces a building on the campus at the University of Illinois and another at Illinois State University. There is also a stone marker across College Avenue from the campus marking the place where he lived and carried out his horticultural experiments.

The second great event of April 1962 was the dedication of Rammelkamp Chapel. At the suggestion of Mrs. Charles Rammelkamp, after whose husband the chapel was named, Dr. Hoskins, chairman of the trustees and then professor of parish ministry at Chicago Theological Seminary, was the main speaker. He, his wife, and both their clergymen sons were graduates of the College. Jacksonville attorney T. C. Rammelkamp '40, son of the former president, spoke for the family. In addition to the Rammelkamp relatives, representatives of the Presbyterian Church and the United Church of Christ, both state and national, were present.

The following month, Mrs. Rammelkamp died at the age of eighty-four. She had been seriously ill for some time, and it was believed that her desire to see the dedication of the chapel honoring her husband gave her the strength to live those last few months. She was a member of the remarkable Capps family, which played such an important role in the lives both of Illinois College and the Jacksonville community for more than a century. Her brother, Stephen '02, was chairman of the Classics Department at Princeton University and ambassador to Greece. One of her sons, Julian '39, was professor of history at Albion College, and another, Charles '33, was on the medical faculty at Western Reserve University and was internationally recognized in medical research.

Mrs. Rammelkamp lived her whole life in Jacksonville. She married young Charles Henry Rammelkamp a few years after he was asked to take over the presidency of Illinois College, then on the verge of collapse. She was no small factor in his brilliant career as president. After his death in 1932, her interest in the College never slackened. In the early 1950s, she was alumni secretary.

I visited her often after I became president. She always stated her views about College matters very forcefully and did not always agree with what I proposed to do. I appreciated her interest and concern but I told her frankly that I would have to use my own best judgment in managing the

The 1960s Begin

Rammelkamp family members at the dedication of the Rammelkamp chapel. *Left to right:* Dr. Julian Rammelkamp '39, Mrs. Edith Rammelkamp Elliott '36, Dr. Charles Henry Rammelkamp, Jr., '33, Mrs. C. H. Rammelkamp, Dr. Joseph Capps '91, Mrs. Rhoda Rammelkamp Bolton '30, Mrs. Stephanie Shambaugh Kramer, Mr. Kramer.

College. We remained on the best of terms. She was a great lady. Her memorial service was the first such exercise held in Rammelkamp Chapel.

As is the case on campuses in general, romance flourishes and chapels are popular sites for weddings. The librarian, C. B. Russell, provided a beautiful marriage book for Rammelkamp Chapel. In April 1962, the first marriage in the chapel

took place. Donna Woodruff '63 and Gale Hurrelbrink '61 were the happy pair. The next three weddings were those of Judith Veith '61 and Ulrich Kuster '61; Palma Reuter '64 and Harold Kund '65; and Linda Lebkuecher '65 and Paul Smith '64.

Noteworthy at Commencement in 1962 was the announcement that the College had received more than the $1,500,000 it had sought to raise when its Forward Step Campaign was announced in 1958. The new Rammelkamp Chapel was completely paid for, and money was on hand for the science hall, already under construction.

4
Growth And Change:
1962–1964

Though nothing looked more peaceful than the campus as college opened in the fall of 1962, it was brought home to us that the world teetered on the brink of the nuclear abyss. During the summer, the Civil Defense Administration had designated the lower floors of Tanner Library and Rammelkamp Chapel as fallout shelters and had stocked them with hermetically sealed cans of water and food. This action was public knowledge, but a secret arrangement also took place.

In response to a request from federal authorities but with the knowledge of only a few of the officials of the College, Tanner Library was made the alternate state headquarters for both the Federal Bureau of Investigation and the Selective Service. Special telephone arrangements were made and desks and typewriters owned by the federal government replaced those of the College. Our own people sat at the desks and used the typewriters for College business, but should Springfield be destroyed, others would take over our facilities. If we wore out a typewriter, we were given a new one to use as we wished—unless Springfield perished.

Two faculty members who joined the staff in the fall of 1962 were to remain. Fred Pilcher succeeded George Horton in the Physics Department. He had a special interest in astronomy and thus added a dimension to the science program. Carole Ann McNamara, winner of the Fulbright scholarship for study in France when she graduated from Illinois College

in 1959, came back from a junior-college position to teach French. While I did not think it a good policy to appoint many alumni to the faculty, an especially good one now and then represented a real asset.

While there was no special financial campaign that year, the total development program of the College was doing well. One aspect of it, begun in 1958, was asking alumni in particular to remember Illinois College in their wills. Quiet personal contacts were best but a letter also was sent out each year to older alumni enclosing a small folder on the subject. During that year, eight wills brought some $250,000 for the general endowment and another endowed a special program. Elzie Weber '09, a country lawyer at Lewistown, a few years before had worked out with me a bequest of $100,000 for the College. He insisted that it should do something for his home county as well as his college, so the income was to become scholarship money for students from Fulton County. The $350,000 added to the endowment that year boosted its total to more than $3,000,000, more than half of which had come in during my administration.

A systematic program for annual gift income also had been developed. The Alumni Fund was much more productive after its revisions. The cooperative annual solicitation of the private colleges of the Associated Colleges of Illinois was working well. CACHE, the joint business solicitation in Jacksonville for both the colleges located here, yielded a modest sum. Money was received indirectly from the Independent Funds of America. The Board of Christian Education of the United Presbyterian Church continued to give sparingly, and its regional counterpart, the General Mission Budget of the Synod of Illinois, was a new supporter. We also were getting our full share of the sporadic support, often through special grants, from the United Church of Christ. Most of these sources were developed during my early days at the College.

For several years, the College had been emphasizing in-

creasing concern for international affairs. Dean Yeager, Dr. Stewart, and I were prime movers. Several faculty members of foreign origin had been appointed and visiting professors from abroad were brought to the campus. The first came by virtue of a Whitney Foundation grant and was shared with MacMurray College. He was Dr. Chun-Suk Auh, former Minister of Education of Korea, who later served his country as ambassador to Mexico. Not only did he teach at the two colleges, he lectured on his country and the problems of Asia all over the area.

The state of Illinois went overboard in plans for higher education. For the ten-year period ending in 1962, the six state universities had increased enrollment by 131 percent. All those new junior colleges had caused an increase of 200 percent in that segment. Private colleges had grown a significant but more modest 56 percent. Although private and tax-supported institutions of higher education had had about the same enrollment, the public institutions now had about twice as many students. With all the indicators pointing to fewer students in the years ahead and with the shift from private to public enrollments, many private colleges failed to heed the signs and dreamed impossible dreams that would lead to financial problems in the years ahead.

That year, William Roosen of Mt. Prospect, a graduating senior, was awarded a Fulbright scholarship for study in France, and Charlotte Thompson Reid '34 joined Paul Findley '43 as a member of Congress.

The Distinguished Visitors Program was well underway. Of the several visitors that fall, two were especially interesting. One, John Beecher, was the great-grandson of the first president of the College and a poet in his own right. An unconventional writer and lecturer, he and his wife roved the country part of the year in a camper and lectured at colleges. He also ran a printing establishment that specialized in artistic printing. He came back to the College a number of times.

Charles Ferguson, an author of some note and a senior editor of *Reader's Digest,* was such a captivating speaker and class leader that we asked him to return in subsequent years.

With a wealth of talent at hand, it was decided that a series of faculty lectures would be inaugurated. This popular feature became a regular annual occurrence. It was managed by a faculty committee that selected the speakers. The first year there were four but later it was reduced to two or three. Among the early speakers was Dr. Hildner, whose topic was "Spain in the Modern World," a report on his sabbatical in Spain where he retraced his path as a graduate student collecting material for his doctoral thesis many years before. Dr. Stewart spoke on "Modern Thailand," based on his recent experience during a sabbatical in that country. Dr. Eleanor Miller's lecture was entitled "Behavioral Science: Threat or Promise." The Whitney Foundation Visiting Professor, Dr. Chun-Suk Auh, gave the fourth lecture. The lecture series was open to the public as well as to faculty and students.

Nearly all of the Commencement speakers were noteworthy for their accomplishments and their messages but some of those during the first half of the decade of the 1960s deserve special mention. In 1961, our speaker was Charles Percy, the "Boy Wonder" of the business world. From humble beginnings, he started his spectacular business career while a student at the University of Chicago. He joined Bell and Howell upon graduation and rose to the presidency of the company by age thirty. Named one of the ten most promising young men of the nation along with John F. Kennedy, he made his company a world leader.

I recall my first meeting with him in Chicago, in part because it was the first time a person had ever sent a chauffeured limousine to pick me up for a luncheon date. His Commencement address was a call for a moral awakening and greater discipline for America.

On that occasion Percy was awarded his first honorary degree. To witness that act, he brought along his wife and

Growth and Change

President Caine confers upon the 1961 Commencement speaker, Charles Percy, the doctor of laws degree.

three of his children, including his teen-aged twin daughters, Valerie and Sharon. The twins were to become front-page news. Valerie's unsolved murder was a national sensation, and Sharon was much in the news when she married Jay Rockefeller, who later became governor of West Virginia.

Within a few years, Percy, having conquered the business world, turned to public service and became a U.S. senator. He stopped at Illinois College frequently. Once when he was on the reelection campaign trail, he dropped in at the office to greet me. He said he was very hot and tired and he wondered if he could go over to our house and take a bath. That was arranged.

The 1962 commencement speaker, J. Edward Day, postmaster general in the Kennedy cabinet, was another interesting person with local connections. He had been born in Jacksonville.

Three new trustees who were to be of special importance

were elected at the spring meeting in 1963. One was Paul Findley, a member of Congress from the Jacksonville district. He was to be especially helpful in getting outstanding talent from government circles to come to the College. The others were Dr. Robert Hartman, who succeeded Dr. Norbury as secretary of the Trustees, and Walter R. Bellatti '36.

A member of the graduating class of 1963, Carol Wilson, Auburn, Massachusetts, was awarded a Fulbright fellowship for a year of study in India. She was the third graduate to receive such an honor in five years.

The dedication of Crispin Science Hall proved to be an added attraction for the 1963 Commencement. Trustee Walter Thwaite provided the distinguished men of science who were the dedication and Commencement speakers. At the ceremonies the day before Commencement, Dr. Calvin A. VanderWerf, chairman of the chemistry department of the University of Kansas and president-elect of Hope College, gave the dedicatory address. A special platform guest was Dr. Willis DeRyke, who had been professor of biology at Illinois College from 1926 to 1953.

The Commencement speaker was one of America's foremost scientists, Dr. James Van Allen, discoverer of the natural radiation belts surrounding the earth, which bear his name. The baccalaureate sermon was given by Dr. Floyd V. Filson, dean of McCormick Theological Seminary and father of Professor Don Filson of our faculty.

That Commencement was also distinguished by the fact that four husband-and-wife couples were members of the graduating class.

The progress of Illinois College, which surpassed everyone's expectations, including mine, did not come easily or automatically. There were agonizing decisions that proved more significant in the long run than they seemed to be at the time. One of the earliest and hardest decisions—as previously discussed—concerned the quality of students. We knew we

Growth and Change

The three oldest alumni attending the alumni luncheon at Commencement 1963. *Left to right:* Dr. William Garret '95, Raymond Ward '89, and C. A. Johnson '97. The first two were present for Commencement on the seventy-fifth anniversary of their graduation in 1972 and 1964, respectively.

were adopting higher standards at great risk. Enrollment was a major problem for a time, but in four years it had increased more than 50 percent.

The decision to put the proceeds of all wills and bequests into the endowment, unless otherwise designated by the donor, was another fortunate move. The fact that such a contribution to the College represents a permanent investment that yields annual returns is a strong factor in encouraging people to make wills benefiting the College.

Another decision that kept Illinois College free from the

troubles that afflicted so many colleges years later was the policy that no building would be constructed unless the money to pay for it was in hand or already pledged. The exception was housing facilities where the income paid off the debt. The loans for the construction of dormitories averaged less than 3.5 percent in interest, and the financial arrangement to retire the debt and pay the interest required the same amount to be paid each year for forty years. While the College was able to pay off these loans much earlier, it did not do so because the money available could be invested at a rate several times that being paid on the loans. Since dormitories were built only as they were needed, the income from them always was more than sufficient to pay operating costs and debt charges. The pay-as-you-go construction policy for other buildings meant that no current income had to be expended to retire debts.

In later years, as a consultant, I came to know how wasteful many small colleges were in their use of space. Presidents were surprised when they learned that many rooms were in use for only five or ten hours per week and that rooms with a capacity of thirty never had a class bigger than twelve meeting in them. Many small colleges could lose from one-third to one-half of their classroom space and still have plenty of room.

While there were many more basic decisions, the most important one was not to bend to every superficial opinion that came along. The principle was to decide what was the best course to follow in the long run and to stick to it. One had to fight to hold to admission standards, to resist constructing buildings that were not needed, to keep high standards of conduct in college living, and to maintain the integrity of liberal education against the inroads of vocationalism. We maintained a conservative stance in a society that was going off in every direction. There were those of the credit-card mentality who would have the College buy now and pay later. I recall a college president friend who had no qualms about

deficits. He said to me once, "Let them have what they want and make them pay for it." Well, they had what they wanted but the college nearly went bankrupt, and he moved on.

It has always been a mystery to me why well educated people are taken by fads in the same manner as those who are less schooled. When one thinks of open classrooms in public elementary schools with children moving about as they please and classes being held in the midst of unstructured turmoil, one wonders now how any responsible educator could have believed it could work. It did not, and the system has gone back to tried and true methods.

We were fortunate that Illinois College did not take any of the attractive but damaging detours that characterized the era. It therefore emerged into the more recent years without the burden of errors and debts that hamper and haunt so many similar institutions (those that survived).

With enrollment increasing substantially every year, the building program was hardly keeping pace with requirements for more space. There was no room for added books and students in the library. After studying the situation, I came up with an idea that would tide us over for a few more years. When Tanner was constructed about thirty-five years before, only the top floor and about one-quarter of the ground floor had been actually used for library purposes. The balance of the building was for administration. Outside the reading room was an ample foyer. By moving the checkout desk and card catalogues to that area, a considerable amount of space was freed for more book shelves. A narrow interior stairway led from the upper-floor stacks to those on the ground floor. By cutting a hole in the floor of the lower stacks and installing a spiral staircase, a stack area of equal dimensions was added on the basement level. Space for books thus was increased by nearly 50 percent. The room adjacent to the newly located checkout desk, formerly the alumni office, became the book accession room. Later, seldom-used books and old bound periodicals were taken out and stored in the upper

story of Whipple Hall. By better utilization of available space we were able to provide adequate library facilities for a few more years while we caught up with other needs. It was apparent that, down the line, a new library would be necessary.

Shortly after the assassination of John F. Kennedy, a delegation of somber students came to our home to make a request. They thought it would be appropriate to have the day of the funeral as a day of mourning on the campus and asked me to call off classes and announce a memorial service for all the College.

I had not yet considered how we should react to this national tragedy. My first reaction, which I expressed to them, was that to take the day off would make it more of a holiday than a solemn occasion and that many of the students would spend their free time in ways that might not be suitable. Their response was that if we did as they suggested they would see to it that the campus was quiet, that all the students would come to the memorial service, and that it would indeed be a day of mourning. I asked them to give me a little time to think it over and promised that I would call their leader within the hour to let them know what I had decided.

Having heard the petition of the students and having observed their sense of desolation over the death of their young national leader, I was inclined to take their suggestion. I decided to seek some advice on the matter. Dr. C. Ellsworth Black, chairman of the Faculty Committee of the trustees, was my next-door neighbor to whom I occasionally turned for advice. He listened to my reasoning and agreed that the wishes of the students should be honored. I informed the student leader and asked them to spread the word about the observance.

In my discussion with the students, they had even suggested some elements of the memorial service, including a main address to be delivered by me. We set up the memorial service and all the students and faculty attended, dressed for church. The campus remained as quiet as vacation all day.

Growth and Change

Most of the students spent the time after the morning service clustered around television sets watching that moving and superb drama of the burial of John F. Kennedy in Arlington National Cemetery. The students were right, and I thanked them for it. That day was not one for college as usual.

Two women of considerable importance in the history of the College retired in the spring of 1964, one from the faculty and the other from the board. Ruth Badger Pixley '18 had been a trustee for thirty years. She and her husband lived in La Jolla, California, and her health no longer permitted her to come to meetings. She had written the words for the alma mater and her husband, Boyd, the music. Their wills would make them the largest of all the College benefactors.

In her letter of resignation, Ruth asked that the board elect a woman as her successor. The choice was Emily Hurd Eppenberger, St. Louis, a civic leader and a national leader in the United Church of Christ where she was serving as vice chairman of the Board of Homeland Ministries.

Dr. Eleanor Miller, chairman of the Department of Psychology, ended her thirty-seven years on the faculty of the College. She was one of the strongest teachers and leaders in the academic community and was active in the affairs of Jacksonville. She would be difficult to replace.

In passing, it should be noted that Illinois College was not guilty of two cardinal sins of American society—discrimination against women and blacks. Blacks had never been denied admission to Illinois College, a center of antislavery sentiment before the Civil War. In this respect, the College was far ahead of its locale. When we first came to Jacksonville, no black man could get a haircut from a white barber; when a black graduate came back for a class reunion, he or she could not find a place to eat or sleep at public accommodations. It is no condemnation of the College that it had never had, up until this time, a black faculty member. None had ever applied. A quiet milestone occurred when Dr. Herman Dreer, a retired professor of long service, replaced Professor

Ruth Bump for a semester. A Phi Beta Kappa, he was the first black person to be a member of the College faculty.

As for discrimination against women, Dr. Ethel Seybold, chairman of the English Department, and Dr. Eleanor Miller, along with Professor George Horton, Physics, were the members of the faculty committee to advise on the selection of a new president when I was hired. Dr. Mary Louise Rainbolt and Professor Carole Ryan headed the Departments of Biology and Modern Languages. Dr. Miller headed the Psychology Department. Thus, women had occupied leadership posts at the College long before the women's movement received national attention in the seventies.

It was gratifying to announce at the semiannual meeting of the trustees in 1963 that faculty salaries had doubled since the beginning of my administration. At a time when inflation was not significant, this increase was a considerable accomplishment.

One of the topics for discussion by the trustees was the retirement age of faculty members. For years it had been sixty-five. Congressman Paul Findley, the successful advocate in Congress of lifting or eliminating a retirement age for jobs of all kinds, brought up the idea of adjusting the retirement age for faculty members. Nothing was done at that meeting but later the age was increased to sixty-eight. It was, in my opinion, a wise action but I would not support increasing it beyond sixty-eight or eliminating it altogether.

Subsequently, it was suggested that there be a retirement age for members of the board. I opposed it and was probably responsible for holding off such an action until my retirement. I had dealt with too many persons who had been among the best trustees, some even in their eighties, to want to lose the older ones. While a considerable number of persons had served during my time as trustees while they were in their upper seventies and lower eighties, only one had failed to retire before his dotage. After I retired, the board set the retirement age for trustees at age seventy-two.

Growth and Change

An unusual situation existed in Jacksonville with respect to electricity. A municipal plant provided part of the requirements but Illinois Power Company also served a good portion of the users. The result was that there were separate lines and twice the number of poles visible in most communities. People or businesses next door to each other would be served by different companies. The College was supplied by the municipal system, which was beginning to deteriorate both in equipment and in service. Frequent power interruptions and low voltage caused many problems. Illinois Power was persistent in applying for our business and promised substantial financial contributions to the College if we would change suppliers. Owing largely to the poor service, the College switched to Illinois Power. The result was much better service and annual contributions from the company. A few years later the municipal plant was sold to Illinois Power.

Another building project was begun with the opening of bids for the swimming-pool addition to Memorial Gymnasium. The cost was something over $200,000. It was a single story high and was attached to the south side of the gymnasium.

A grant from the U.S. Steel Foundation, conditional upon the College raising a matching funds—which was rapidly accomplished—provided the equipment for the science hall.

The first Joe Patterson Smith Lecture was given in the spring of 1964, with Dr. Gordon Craig, a historian from Stanford University, as the speaker. Congressman Paul Findley was a speaker who lectured at the College at least once a year during my presidency.

The variety of instructional visitors who were willing to come to the College at their own expense to speak and to teach was remarkable. One of the most flamboyant was long remembered by some. At least fifteen years later, an unusually successful businessman who as a student heard W. Clement Stone, the multimillionaire rags-to-riches insurance magnate, at a College convocation, told me that that occa-

sion was one of the most memorable and significant incidents in his college career. I recall visiting Stone in Chicago and asking him to come down. He agreed readily and brought along a truckload of books, including copies of one or two he had written. The theme of all of them was that nothing is impossible to achieve if you really go after it. He used himself as an example. Every student and faculty member at the College received four volumes. Stone's evangelical fervor was a source of wonder, admiration, and for some, amusement.

Governor Kerner, whom I had come to know rather well, accepted an invitation to speak at a convocation. His visit occurred only a few weeks after the assassination of President Kennedy and greater precautions were being taken to safeguard high public officials. The day before the governor was to speak, a security man came to discuss arrangements and to inspect the places where the governor would appear; previously, the governor had traveled only with a state police driver. The governor delivered a fine speech and was a delightful guest at our home, where some fifty or sixty people had gathered for lunch. Good at public relations, he went out in the kitchen after the meal to thank the help for their services.

I knew a number of Illinois governors but I had more to do with Kerner than with any others (even though he was not of my political persuasion). On several occasions, Elizabeth and I, or I alone, were guests at the Governor's Mansion. Some of the visits were connected with the Lincoln Academy, which he inaugurated to honor great people of Illinois. I was a trustee. At an annual meeting of the academy, famous people who were born in or had worked in Illinois were invested at a special service. At first, these gatherings were held in Chicago, but later the event was moved to Springfield and took place in the Old Capitol. An elaborate dinner was always part of the proceedings.

Included among those persons I met in this connection were three or four Nobel Prize winners, several members of

Growth and Change

Governor Otto Kerner, sitting in the Abraham Lincoln chair, looks at a historic scrapbook in President Caine's office.

presidents' cabinets, great sports figures, cartoonists such as Al Capp, and singers such as Pearl Bailey.

One luncheon at the Governor's Mansion stands out in my mind. About two days before, I had received a call informing

me that Austria's Minister of Education was coming to the United States to receive an honorary degree from Harvard University. He was an Abraham Lincoln buff and was taking the opportunity to extend his visit to Springfield to see the Lincoln sites. Governor Kerner was entertaining him at a luncheon and thought it would be proper to have an educator or two in the luncheon party so I was invited. Nine men sat down at the governor's table with the host at the end, the minister to his right, and I next to him. The conversation was fascinating. Both the governor and the minister had commanded units in World War II and they discovered that they had fought directly against each other in one operation.

I liked and admired Governor Kerner and was shocked and distressed when it was discovered that he had taken bribes. He was a most gracious person and unsurpassed in tact and civility. He attracted national attention as the chairman of the presidential commission that issued the famous Kerner Report on integration. It was tragic that so able and charming a man should die in disgrace.

A highlight of the year was a three-week long exhibit of Leonardo da Vinci's models and inventions. The exhibit had first been constructed in 1936 but was destroyed in the bombing of Tokyo during World War II. Restored by an Italian da Vinci scholar, it was acquired by IBM and exhibited in such places as the New York Metropolitan Museum of Art and the Chicago Museum of Science. Large crowds, including busloads of students from a wide area, viewed the exhibition.

Illinois College was also the site of the annual selection of candidates for the United States military academies. Congressman Paul Findley delegated the selection of those from this congressional district to boards of citizens who interviewed all the candidates. More than fifty applicants would be interviewed by selection committees for each of the academies.

Along about this time, Illinois College scored one of its

Growth and Change

Under the direction of Professor Raymond Ford, the College continued its tradition of superiority in forensics. Here Ford talks to John Betonte *(left)* and James Reilly *(center)* as they depart for the Harvard Invitational Debate Tournament in 1964. They were undefeated in seven rounds but lost to Northwestern University, the eventual winner, in the semifinals. Betonte went on to become senior vice president of one of America's largest oil brokerage firms and Reilly became a member of the Illinois General Assembly until he accepted the appointment of chief of staff for Governor Thompson.

greatest athletic triumphs in the last game of the football season. Up against Washington University of St. Louis, rated eleventh among the nonmajor teams of the nation, the Blueboys managed a touchdown in the first half and a safety later and held on for a 9–7 win in a major upset. What was supposed to be a 4–4 season ended up with 5 wins and 3 losses.

In the latter days of 1955, when I was pondering the offer to become president of Illinois College, one of the institution's positive factors was its athletic philosophy. I had al-

ways been deeply interested in sports and had coached high school basketball for five years. I was and am convinced that playing on a team is a valuable experience and a proper intercollegiate program is a great asset to a college. At the same time I was unalterably opposed to offering financial inducements as a recruiting practice. Illinois College did not give aid to students for being athletes but only on the basis of need. If there was a conflict between team and academic obligations, the latter responsibilities took precedence.

The management of intercollegiate athletics was in accord with the best traditions of liberal education. A faculty committee was in charge, and their actions had to be confirmed by the whole faculty. Another faculty committee, Admissions, saw to it that athletes measured up to academic requirements and were treated the same as other students when it came to financial assistance. The system went unchanged during my administration.

But football was in deep trouble at Illinois College. In his June 1955 annual report to the trustees, President Selden said it was likely that the College would have to abandon football for lack of sufficient players. With enrollment well below the 300 mark, not enough men came out for football. In the fall of 1956 and 1957, there were times when it was not possible to have a full scrimmage; one side of the line would have to play against the other side in practice sessions.

Even though the numbers were small, the teams were doing quite well. Track had just been revived after a dozen years, and in basketball, football, and baseball, 1954–1955 was not a bad year overall. The record in football was only 2 wins and 7 losses, but basketball was 13 and 7 while baseball was 9 and 7. Selden had reported that there had been only 20 men out for football with only 16 able to participate. Only 11 would return, and the fate of football would rest on the number of newcomers who chose to play. Surprisingly, enough came and the 1955 season ended with a record of 4 wins, a loss, and a tie.

Growth and Change

Except for basketball, there was not much in the way of athletic facilities. Football was played on the high-school field and baseball in the northwest corner of the campus with home plate situated in the Ames Woodlawn Theater next to Beecher Hall, whose windows were alarmingly vulnerable to foul balls. The left fielder had to run up and down a sharp slope next to the driveway of the president's house.

When I saw the basketball team in action for the first time in late January of 1956, I thought they were pretty good. They were. It turned out to be a 17 win–7 loss season. One of the impressive seniors was William Merris, who a few years later became the coach. He also was the All-Prairie Conference catcher that spring when the baseball team won 9 of their 19 games.

In the second season for track, two men, Ogden Munroe and Gary Turpin, were first place winners in four of the five meets. Turpin became a physician and Munroe a dentist.

World War II and the returning GIs had disrupted traditional athletic programs and things only were returning to normal by the mid–1950s. Track had been revived in 1955 and tennis and golf in 1956.

The 1956–1957 football team won 2 of 7 games and the manpower shortage was apparent, for only 17 men won letters. The basketball team won 10 of 25, but 2 of their losses were in overtime and the opponents included Western Illinois, Earlham, Austin, and Washington University. The track team won one quadrangular meet, the new tennis team lost all its matches, and the golf team won the conference championship. The College was competing in five sports plus riflery, and the outlook was better. All the coaching was done by Joe Brooks. Women's physical education and intramural sports were under the direction of a part-time faculty member.

It became apparent that improved athletic facilities must be included in any plans for progress at the College. The local school district was building a new junior high school and the

preferred site was part of the College campus. Across the street south of the gymnasium, a block-wide strip of land sloped downward about three blocks. It was a rather rough piece of land. At the south end, the College cemetery had been located in the earliest days of the institution. At some time in the intervening century, the burials were supposed to have been transferred to other cemeteries. The school district wanted the lower end of the tract for the new junior high school.

The College was badly in need of money and agreed in 1954 to sell the south end to the school district for $21,800, with the stipulation that a certain part of the fund would be used to develop some of the adjacent college-owned land for use by both institutions for playing fields. Beginning in 1956 and over several years, the College developed excellent facilities for outdoor sports including a football field with a track around it, a baseball diamond, and a practice field. All the fields were tiled and much grading was required to make each of them level. Some friction developed over use of the fields by junior-high-school children and a friendly termination of their use by the school was arranged.

The football field was not properly sodded and ready for play until 1959, when it was first used in a thrilling game with Central Methodist College. Illinois College came from behind to win 32 to 26. By the following spring, the baseball diamond and the track were ready for use.

In 1965, Mrs. Marian French '31, an ardent fan and a wonderful supporter of athletes, took the lead in a drive that produced a brick press box located over a refreshment stand and storage space. A fine electric scoreboard and flagpole were installed at the south end of the field.

As for the coaching duties, few colleges have had less turnover. When I came upon the scene, Al Miller was Athletic Director and coach of about half the teams. Joe Brooks was a half-time teacher and coach with the balance of his time taken as Dean of Men. Miller resigned suddenly just before

college opened in the fall of 1956. Brooks became the Director of Athletics and coached basketball, football, and baseball. With a little part-time help, he took care of the other sports and the Physical Education Department. In 1958, William Merris '56 joined the staff as basketball coach. In 1973, Tom Rowland '69, one of the College's all-time great football players, became the third full-time man in the department.

The win-loss record through the rest of the 1950s was not particularly impressive. In only one year did the football team lose more games than it won. In half of the basketball seasons, the record was 50–50 and the rest below. Baseball had one winning season, and only once did tennis reach the break-even point. Wrestling emerged but faded away after two seasons. The track teams were about average, but there were some excellent individual winners. With the completion of the new swimming pool, aquatics became an intercollegiate activity. Before World War II, the College had had some fine swimming teams, using the pool at the School for the Deaf.

In 1960–1961, MacMurray's College for Men fielded its first basketball team. Having used all sorts of financial inducements to get men to come to what had been a women's college and having decided not to develop a football program, they spared no expense to recruit good basketball players. Their aspirations were to compete at a much more prestigious level than Illinois College ever hoped or desired to reach. In their earlier years, MacMurray developed its best teams, and at a later time had to be satisfied with playing the usual run of small colleges in the area.

While neither Illinois College nor MacMurray really wanted to play each other, community pressures seemed to make it inevitable; it was agreed that there would be a home-and-home series every year. The largest crowds either team played before attended games in those first years. In fact, MacMurray once moved its home game to the high school bowl to allow more spectators to attend.

In the first few years, Illinois College players were no match for the men MacMurray recruited, and it was not until years later, when economic factors and a less aggressive coach produced a team more representative of the size and nature of their college, did Illinois College begin to make a reasonable showing.

Tension ran high in the first few games. In order to keep the competition among the fans as moderate as possible, the two presidents decided they would sit together at the game, the first half on one side, and the second on the other. As time went on, the tension at game-time gradually lessened. Crowds diminished and the big game provoked only mild rivalry between two neighbors.

In that first year, Illinois College lost the first game 69 to 59 and the second 100 to 84. And MacMurray kept on winning year after year. In 1962–1963, a game went into overtime but MacMurray won. It was not until 1966–1967 that Illinois College won its first game and not until my last year that we won both. An ardent fan, I had the miserable experience of sitting through game after game, having to congratulate MacMurray on winning.

There are many great stories of athletic victories and defeats over the years. In 1965, Principia defeated Illinois College in a baseball game that lasted four and one-half hours and ended with the score 36 to 23. Illinois College defeated Culver-Stockton 18 to 12 later that same season. It was not a pitcher's year.

It is unlikely that many alumni or close friends are aware that Illinois College once won a national athletic championship and had a man on an All-American team. It happened in 1959. Robert Hickey in his senior year won the 1959 National Intercollegiate Rifle Championship and was named to the eight-man All American Rifle team. He also set a new national record of 299 out of 300 bullseyes and was so certified by the National Rifle Association.

5
Golden Years: 1964–1967

In 1964–1965 the face of the campus was changed. The College borrowed $600,000 at 3.75 percent interest from the Department of Housing and Urban Development to construct another dormitory for men and an addition to Baxter Dining Hall. Both projects were completed in time for the opening of the 1965–1966 academic year.

The new residence hall, named in honor of the legendary Jonathan Baldwin Turner, was erected on the site of Russell House, which had been demolished. This frame structure had come into the possession of the College as a result of the settlement of the bank defalcation in 1932 and had been used for many purposes over the intervening years. It was in poor condition and not worth keeping.

Baxter Hall was as sound as ever but too small to accommodate the growing student body. The enlargement was done in a most ingenious manner. Since the upper story was supported by the walls of the building rather than pillars, it was not possible to remove any walls. On the south side of the dining room were several sets of double windows. By removing the windows and the wall above and below, at least half the entire wall was gone. These openings allowed unhindered access to the new addition. The kitchen was placed in the lower floor, which was below ground on one side and at ground level on the other. The entire building was reequipped and a serviceable and attractive facility resulted.

Then there was Federal Hall, a World War II surplus build-

ing the size of a tennis court and one story high, in which classes and faculty offices were situated. It was located between old Jones and new Ellis. When the GI Bill student influx took place, practically every college and university in America took advantage of the offer of free temporary buildings from war training camps; many were used for married students' housing and others for classrooms. At Illinois College, many of the housing units had been demolished as they became dilapidated. A few remained for storage. Federal Hall was now in bad shape and no longer needed; it was demolished that year. The cement slab on which it stood became a tennis court.

To make up for the seven classrooms and eight faculty offices lost, the lower floor of Rammelkamp Chapel was divided into rooms and Tanner and Whipple were renovated. Eighteen new classrooms and fifteen new offices resulted. That year, 1965, a language laboratory was also opened in Crispin Hall. The campus now had the facilities to teach 800 students.

This was a year of spectacular enrollment increase. Total registration went up by 18 percent, owing largely to a 63 percent increase in the size of the freshman class. We could have used the new dormitory that was being constructed because Gardner, Crampton, and Fayerweather could not house all the men nor could we place all the women in Ellis and Colonial Inn. It was necessary to find rooms in area homes for a considerable number of students. With the opening of Turner the following fall, the men gave up Fayerweather to the women.

Two newcomers were added to the faculty and stayed on beyond my retirement. They were Dr. Louis Meek in psychology and Ts'ing Hi-Tong in mathematics.

The College now had its own band. Years before, MacMurray and Illinois College had had a joint band. The opening of MacMurray's College for Men terminated that arrangement and opened a new era for music at Illinois Col-

lege, which surpassed previous offerings. Music and art at Illinois College occupied a lesser place than at most liberal arts colleges for many years and for good reasons. Back in 1871, the Conservatory of Music was established in Jacksonville. It later merged with the Jacksonville Female Academy, which was founded at the same time as Illinois College and was somewhat related. During President Clifford Webster Barnes's administration (1905), the academy merged with the College to make a coeducational institution.

The conservatory faculty shifted over to the Female Academy at the time of their merger. It occupied the building that later was torn down to make way for the high-school athletic bowl in the 1950s. The conservatory became too much of a drain on the resources of the academy and an agreement was made that for a certain number of years all music teaching would be done by the Illinois Women's College (MacMurray). If students at Illinois College wanted to take music, they could take it at MacMurray College and apply the credits at Illinois College. The joint band was a natural outgrowth of this arrangement.

Although the expiration date of the arrangement had passed, Illinois College had not begun to offer music courses to any extent. When I arrived on the scene there was a single music class that was required for all persons who planned to teach in elementary schools. It was taught on the Illinois campus by a member of the MacMurray faculty. A chapel choir, under the direction of Mrs. Walter Bellatti, a former MacMurray faculty member, had been started. A few students went to MacMurray to take other music courses.

Art offerings were at a minimum also. Some students interested in art took classes at MacMurray. Conflicting schedules often prevented students from taking more music or art courses.

Illinois College's art and music offerings were predicated on the belief that both were an essential part of a liberal education. It did not have sufficient offerings for those who

had art or music as a major or even as a minor field of study. To do even the minimum and to permit participation in vocal and instrumental college groups, some expansion of the faculty was necessary. It was essential also to offer certain courses needed for the training of elementary teachers.

When additional teaching help in English became necessary, John Specht, who had good credentials in both music and English, was appointed to teach in both fields. An energetic and enthusiastic young man, he was responsible for some important advancements in music. He took a student pep band and made it into a good all-purpose college organization, he enlarged the choir, and he installed new vitality into some additional courses in music.

The musical renaissance was enhanced greatly by the gifts of Mrs. Frank F. Byrom, residing in Palm Beach, Florida. Mrs. Byrom, in 1960, had equipped each dormitory with a television set. Now she contributed $1,000 for new band instruments, and later she purchased about everything the band needed except the individual instruments owned by students. For good measure, she paid for risers for the choir.

The art situation was improved in a rather novel way. Years before, a so-called cattle king, Jacob Strawn, had amassed a fortune and built a palatial home a half mile from the campus. This fine building came into the possession of the Jacksonville Art Association, which had inadequate funding to carry on a program and to maintain the property. An agreement was reached with the Art Association for Illinois College to employ a full-time art instructor. Half of his or her salary would come from the association and teaching time would be divided equally between the two institutions. It was a good arrangement for both parties. Thus, the College strengthened its minimal offerings in art.

While not a college event, the celebration of the 125th anniversary of the founding of the firm of J. Capps and Sons deserves mention because the family has been so closely associated with Illinois College for such a long time. The foun-

der, Joseph Capps, left his father's plantation in Kentucky during President Edward Beecher's administration to come to Jacksonville because of his antislavery convictions. His son Stephen graduated from Illinois College in 1857, and since that time an unbroken succession of family members has been a part of campus life.

The company began spinning wool and making blankets and men's furnishings. They were the outfitters for the Buffalo Bill Wild West Show. In later years, they manufactured men's suits, slacks, jackets, and overcoats. Their lines of clothing bore such names as "Beecher Hall." The marriage of Jeanette Capps to President Rammelkamp, mentioned elsewhere, was another strong link with the College. Robert M. Capps '17, vice president of the College trustees and president of the company, was on the board when I came and continued in both capacities until his death a few years later. After his passing, the company fell upon hard times and was liquidated.

A special event on the campus that fall was the annual meeting of the Federation of Illinois Colleges and Universities. This organization was composed of thirty-one private institutions including most of the colleges and such universities as Chicago, Northwestern, and Loyola. The purpose was to promote the interests of private higher education, including working with the legislature. At that meeting, President George W. Beadle of the University of Chicago reported that the new scholarship program helped pay the expenses of 4500 students and that 35 percent of the aid went to students at private institutions. It was at this meeting that the decision was made to hire a full-time director for the federation. A much talked-about and long-remembered feature of the meeting was the annual dinner that, for the only time in my experience, was held at the home of the president, not in a commercial establishment.

Another event of the year was the periodic inspection and evaluation of the College by the North Central Association

of which Illinois College was a charter member and by which it had been fully accredited since 1915. The most important benefit to the College was the involvement of the total faculty and administration in filling out the evaluation forms covering every aspect of the institution.

As the final act in the exercise, the dean and the president appeared at a meeting of the Accreditation Committee in Chicago to explain or to defend their institution. Dean Yeager and I had little more to do than spend a few pleasant moments with the committee, which passed the institution with flying colors.

This was the first year in its history that the budget of the College went over the $1 million mark. Only six years earlier it had passed for the first time the $500,000 mark. The increase was attributable to growth, not to inflation.

In consideration of the progress of the College, the board directed the publication of a report on the first decade of the Caine administration. This promotional piece, a sixteen-page letter-sized booklet, cited the fact that there had been $2.5 million worth of construction, more than $1 million had been added to the endowment, all past debts had been paid, and the enrollment had doubled. The assets of the College had increased by 115 percent, the size of the faculty by 50 percent, and the amount spent on instruction by 180 percent. The operating budget had been balanced every year.

The nontangible improvements included the switch to machine accounting, the institution of a sabbatical leave system for the faculty, greatly increased fringe benefits, the establishment of a faculty travel fund, the establishment of the Distinguished Visitors and Far Eastern Scholar programs and a better-trained faculty—more than half of whom had their doctorates and others on the way to achieving that degree.

A word about foreign students at Illinois College is appropriate. While foreign students had been a part of the campus life of many institutions for generations, a veritable flood of them came to this country after World War II. In later years,

Golden Years

these students had a greater tendency to congregate on larger campuses, but during the decades of the fifties and sixties most liberal arts colleges had significant representations.

Illinois College welcomed students from many lands. The number at any one time was never large—six or eight in any one year. In 1955–1956, Lebanon, Indonesia, Korea, Thailand, and Japan were represented in the student body. In general, these young men and women were very able people, although often deficient in English. Some were refugees. Many came over under missionary auspices and almost all with substantial assistance in the form of scholarship aid. Those students from countries under Communist domination were not required to go back when their education was finished; many chose to stay in America.

In later years, I began to doubt the wisdom of bringing some of the best minds from struggling nations to be educated in America on the theory that they would return and help raise the level of life in their home lands. They usually stayed in America and their nations were the poorer for the loss. For example, I never knew a Korean student at this college, or in the others where I served, to return home.

One Asian student who did return to his native land was Amnuay Tapingkae, a wonderful Christian young man from Thailand. He received his degree from Illinois College in 1959 and was active in the Presbyterian Church. He went on to earn a doctorate and returned to Thailand to become a leading Far East educator. Now president of Payap College in Chiang Mai, Thailand, he formerly was head of a Far East Institute in Singapore.

Yasuko Ogishima, who came from Japan in 1960, had an excellent mind and unbounded determination—but inadequate English. My wife Elizabeth, a friend to all students, saw that she needed love and attention and provided it. Yasuko was a frequent visitor at our home. She did poorly her first semester, and an investigation revealed that she stayed up almost all night working on her subjects because she could

not read English fast enough. At our insistence, Yasuko dropped a course and was given help to do better in the others. She proceeded to learn rapidly and graduated an honor student. Yasuko went to graduate school in library science at the University of Illinois and married a fellow countryman who was doing graduate work there. We attended their wedding. Today, her husband is a professor at Yale University, and she is a member of the staff of the Metropolitan Museum in New York City. As a token of appreciation, Yasuko made us a wreath for her last Christmas before graduation. It is an intricate and beautiful decoration that I display every Christmas.

One of the experiences I like to recount for the amusement of friends, although it was no laughing matter for me at the time, had to do with one of my frequent trips. Along with about 200 others in leadership roles through the nation, I had been invited by the State Department to a briefing on foreign policy in Washington. We were to spend a long day in the State Department hearing officials justify our policy toward the Soviet Union and the Viet Nam War.

Experience had taught me the wisdom of taking along as little luggage as possible when traveling. I drove to Springfield with a single medium-sized bag, and, since I was to be gone only two nights for the one-day meeting, I wore the only suit I was taking. The parking lot at the airport was dark, and in my rush to catch the plane I stumbled and fell to my knees. The fall cut a substantial triangular tear in the knee of my trousers.

I arrived in Washington about midnight and found only a drug store open. Since we were required to be at the State Department by eight o'clock in the morning and no stores were open at that hour, I had to make do with what I had. I bought a roll of white tape, and used it on the underside of the material to restore the cloth to its original place, and with a ball-point pen, made the white that shone through dark enough to almost hide the patching job.

Golden Years

President and Mrs. Caine and their cat, a campus character.

The next morning I arrived at the meeting place, carrying a briefcase strategically located to conceal the repair. I met many of the leaders, including Secretary of State Dean Rusk and others who made foreign policy. It was announced at our noon luncheon that President Lyndon Johnson and Vice President Hubert Humphrey would attend the reception held for us at the end of the day. At the appointed time, we were taken to the reception room where there were refreshments. Humphrey arrived first and made a short speech (the only short one I ever heard him give). Having known him for many years through South Dakota and Minnesota associations, we had a chance to renew our acquaintance. President Johnson arrived and, after brief remarks, circulated among us. I literally rubbed elbows with him and still remember how long his arms were and how thin his wrists.

All this time I was carrying my brief case as if it contained state secrets and always, as I talked to people, I kept it in front of the wounded knee of my pants. When the meeting ended, I hurried to a clothing store and was fortunate to be able to find a pair of trousers that matched my coat and were of the right length. At last I looked presentable, now that it did not matter.

A college president must attend a great many meetings outside the community. One of the annual gatherings I enjoyed most was that of the Association of American Colleges, the liberal arts section of higher education. Some of the meetings were of historic consequences. I recall the vigorous battle over whether or not private colleges should accept government grants for academic purposes. In the early stages, I was against it but was eventually overruled. I enjoyed three years of service on the International Relations Committee of the association.

For years, the meetings of the college denominational groups were held in conjunction with the association's annual meetings. I was president of a college related to both the Presbyterian and the Congregational Churches. I was twice

elected president of the Congregational group and served as its secretary for several years. And I was a member of the Nexus Committee for the Presbyterians and served on the committee that set up the Presbyterian scholarship system.

The Roman Catholic colleges had a strong organization that exerted considerable influence in educational matters. As a balancing force, a Protestant group was organized. It lasted for only six or eight years and then disbanded.

The most useful series of meetings I attended during my presidency was that of a completely unofficial group. Earl McGrath, who formed the group and ran it, was one of the most significant figures of my day in higher education. The product of a Lutheran college, Dr. McGrath was at that time director of the Institute of Higher Education, Teachers College, Columbia University. He had been president of the University of Buffalo and was the U.S. Commissioner of Education in the Eisenhower administration.

Dr. McGrath was convinced that church-related colleges were an essential component of American higher education and that their future was threatened by the dilution of purpose and the failure of many of them to carry out their historic mission. He arbitrarily called together about twenty-five presidents of colleges representing a variety of denominations to think through some of the major issues of our times. The meetings were held first at a mansion owned by Columbia University, up the Hudson River from New York. We also met at a lodge in the Poconos in Pennsylvania a few times and other places as well.

While the presidents who were invited were usually not the same each year, I had the privilege of attending every meeting. Dr. McGrath always had as a special guest for the three days a major world thinker in the area of our concern. There were not only lectures and discussions but plenty of opportunity to chat with the visitors and among ourselves. The results of questionnaires filled out by each college before the meetings became discussion topics.

The 1965 Commencement was especially memorable for several reasons. It was the first time in the history of the College that the graduating class had been 100 or more in size. There were 115 graduates. With the larger lower classes, that number continued to grow until the year of my retirement, when it was about 190.

The Commencement speaker was special also. He was four-star General Harold K. Johnson, Chief of Staff of the U.S. Army. As a young officer in the Philippines when World War II broke out, he survived the Bataan Death March and spent the war as a Japanese prisoner. While Congressman Paul Findley was largely responsible for the fact that General Johnson was the Commencement speaker, I had many connections with him also. He was a native of North Dakota, where I lived for a considerable period of time, so we had mutual acquaintances. His wife was from Aberdeen, South Dakota, the state in which I had spent my early teaching years; I was familiar with her family. She had two brothers who were great football players at the University of Minnesota, which I had also attended.

It is interesting to note those who were honored at the 1965 Commencement. In addition to General Johnson there were two other men and a woman. The latter was Frances McReynolds Smith '33, State Department officer for Australia, New Zealand, and the islands of the South Pacific. The others were the president of the Midwest Stock Exchange, James Day, and Milburn Akers, a native of Jacksonville and editor of the Chicago *Sun-Times*. Akers was the major spokesman for private higher education in its successful effort to pass legislation providing funds for private colleges in Illinois.

The recipients of alumni citations were hardly less significant. Dr. and Mrs. George H. Garrison, presidents of the Oklahoma Medical Association and its auxiliary, were two of them. The others were General Robert B. Miller '36, commander of a division of the Strategic Air Command, John

Shepherd '49, president of the Missouri Bar Association, and Mrs. Charlotte Thompson Reid, who rose to fame as the soloist for the nationally known radio program, "Don McNeil's Breakfast Club," and who was now a member of Congress.

During Commencement Week, a dinner was held for a unique person in the history of the College, Leo "Doc" O'Brien. He was a bachelor who owned a large home on Mound Avenue, and over the years he had provided living quarters, other assistance, and advice to more than 200 young men while they attended Illinois College. More than 100 of his "boys" and their wives paid tribute to "Doc" at the dinner.

Important developments marked the opening of the 1965–1966 college year. There was the dedication of the new dormitory for men, Turner Hall, and the opening of the greatly enlarged Baxter Dining Hall. Turner cost $400,000 and housed 107 students.

Aid to students from state and federal sources had been handled, before this time, by the Business Office with the help of Admissions. It had begun with the distribution of only a few thousand dollars and was in time to reach more than $1 million. The Business Office could no longer take care of the processing of applications and making awards. Philip Bradish '29, former Morgan County Clerk, was appointed as the first Financial Aid Director.

The second new officer was one of the most fortunate appointments of my administration. To assist in administrative matters, Lawrence G. Bienert, a clergyman who had been manager of his Baptist denominational bookstore in Chicago, became assistant to the president. His duties included public relations and management of campus events. While he was not a fund raiser, he kept the records of contributions, the area in which the president was in charge. He was efficient, effective, and well liked.

That fall marked the beginning of the Visiting Asian Pro-

fessors Program, which was to continue for many years. My belief that the College should expose students to other cultures was supported by many of the faculty and particularly by Dean Yeager and Professor Malcolm Stewart who coordinated the program. The College already offered a few courses in the field: world religions; some ancient, Near East, and Greek history; world literature; and comparative government. Three competent Asian scholars, Professors Tong, Chien, and Singh, were regular members of the faculty. A little earlier, the College had been fortunate enough to have Dr. Auh, former Minister of Education of Korea, and later ambassador to Mexico, spend a year on the campus under a grant we had obtained. His presence only whetted our appetite for more people like him.

In seeking ways to extend the international impact on the campus, we discovered that the Fulbright program, along with the Asia Foundation and the State Department, was bringing Asian scholars to the United States so that they might learn first hand how our system worked. All were members of faculties in their native countries and were to teach here also. We applied for a place in the program and were included. At first, an Asian scholar was assigned to each campus for a full semester but later for only half a semester. For a time we shared our scholars with MacMurray College, and we also acted as a sponsoring agency in working out arrangements for a number of midwestern colleges to be included.

Each visitor taught a course that had to do with the history, culture, literature, religion, and politics of his or her nation. They also had opportunities to teach in the fields of their specialty. In addition, each of them spoke to organizations of every kind in Jacksonville and the surrounding area.

The first scholar was an Indian from Kashmir and the second was from the Philippines. Others were from China, Burma, Japan, Nepal, and Korea. Several, at intervals, were from the same nation. Dr. Stewart, whose heart was in the

program, did an excellent job of coordinating. I regarded this rather extensive program as one of the finest educational and cultural features of my administration.

Illinois College did its part to encourage ecumenism after Pope John XXIII opened the way for greater cooperation between the Roman Catholic Church and Protestantism. A day-long conference called "Conversations in Ecumenism" was held on the campus under our sponsorship with two professors from seminaries, one Roman Catholic and the other Protestant, as leaders. Clergy of various denominations, including many priests and nuns, participated. I could not help but recall that only a few years before I had invited a Catholic priest to conduct a chapel service at the College. He was not permitted to so do by his bishop. Now, here in Rammelkamp Chapel, nuns, priests, and Protestant clergy of several denominations were discussing basic issues of faith and works—something that had not often happened since the Reformation.

Among the special visitors during the year was an alumnus who had distinguished himself in a special way. William Walton '31, an artist of some renown, was then chairman of the Fine Arts Commission appointed by President Kennedy. He had been Kennedy's campaign manager in Wisconsin and was a personal friend of both the president and his wife. He not only went through the now standard procedure of lectures, conferences, and service club appearances but also gave the College one of his paintings, entitled *Rally*, which had been inspired by the Kennedy presidential campaign. While in Jacksonville, he stayed at the home of his sister, Mrs. Helen Hackett '27.

An incident relating to Walton, which occurred later, is worth recounting. An English artist who was a friend of our artist son, Alan, came to America on a grant to visit art centers. He stopped off in Jacksonville to visit us, and I told him about Bill Walton. He expressed a desire to talk with Bill when he went to Washington. Walton was willing to see

him. At the same time Walton had advertised an apartment in his home for rent. One day there was a knock on Walton's door, and a young man appeared whom Walton thought was our English friend. Walton had shown him the studio and some of his own works when the young man broke in with the question, "All this is very nice, but where is my room?"

Trustee emeritus Ruth Badger Pixley died that year. She had been a valued member of the board for thirty years before her retirement in 1964. She and her husband had made a joint will that, ten years later, resulted in an increase in the endowment of the College by nearly $1,250,000, the largest gift ever made to the College.

The growing faculty and some replacements included four people who would stay on as long as I did. One was Edgar Franz, who came from Culver-Stockton College to bring order and distinction to the Mathematics Department, which had been floundering for a few years. George Mann joined the Physics Department and taught mathematics as well. Dr. Rainbolt took charge of the Biology Department, and Elizabeth Zeigler, whose husband was a business executive, came to teach political science.

The enrollment increased by about 100, and the second largest freshman class in the history of the College up to the time of my retirement was enrolled. (The largest was in 1970.) We seemed to be one of the few colleges that was aware, through population statistics and other factors, that college enrollment was soon to reach its peak, making growth a thing of the past.

The year 1965–1966 was a good one for athletics. The football team, with a 6–2 record, had one of its best seasons. The College won the Prairie Conference championships in football, basketball, and tennis, and for the first time the basketball team went into the NAIA district playoffs.

A unique and unprecedented event was a major exhibit by one of America's foremost artists, Thomas Hart Benton. Lyle S. Woodcock '33, a St. Louis businessman, was a good friend

Golden Years

of the artist and owned a number of his works. He arranged for Benton to loan a considerable number of his works for a weeklong exhibit and to come to the College to lecture. Benton suffered a heart attack shortly before the date of the lecture, and so Woodcock filled in for him. The cost of the exhibit, including transportation, insurance, and the beautifully printed programs, were a gift to the College.

The works in the display were, at that time, worth about half a million dollars. One of them had occupied the central position in the museum display at the New York World's Fair. The exhibit was placed in the lounge of Turner Hall and student guards were on duty every hour of the day and night. Hundreds of people, including busloads of schoolchildren, crowded in to see the exhibit. It was the most important event of its kind ever held on the campus. At the conclusion of the exhibit, two lithographs from the display were presented to the College. One was hung in the president's office and the other in the president's home.

The program of distinguished visitors who spoke at convocations and led classes was in high gear that year. DeWitt Wallace, founder and publisher of *Reader's Digest*, had agreed to send us some national figures beginning that fall. The first was Dr. Walter Judd, famous medical missionary to China and later a member of Congress from Minnesota. George McGovern was the Joe Patterson Smith lecturer.

Under the direction of Professor Tong, the beginnings of a computer program appeared. He taught a single course about computers, and the College secured computer time at the University of Missouri at Rolla and at the Argonne Laboratory.

Some years before, the College had adopted a policy of permitting freshmen to be excused from the first year of English if they could pass a proficiency test. Few had opted for exemption. A new plan was adopted whereby freshmen with excellent high-school grades in English and with high scores in college entrance tests would go directly into second-

semester English; these students would receive credit for their first semester provided their work in English 102 was of high quality. This was an example of the excellent work of the Educational Policies Faculty Committee under the leadership of Dean Yeager.

That Illinois College was receptive to nontraditional educational experiences for its students is indicated by the fact that three students had spent the previous year in studies abroad and had now returned for their senior year at Illinois College. Alta Linnenburger had been in Germany and Susan Kinchloe in France. Julia Campbell went to Puerto Rico for her junior year.

In the spring of 1966, the College suffered a serious loss in the sudden death of the chairman of the board, Dr. Fred Hoskins. One of the College's most distinguished alumni, he had been a member of the board since 1953. When Harry Dunbaugh relinquished the chairmanship in 1955 because of age, Dr. Hoskins was selected to succeed him. He had been a wise and constructive leader during the critical days when the College was getting itself together after the difficulties of the early 1950s. He had much to do with restoring better relationships between the College and both the Congregational and Presbyterian Churches.

At the time of his election to the chairmanship, Dr. Hoskins was the pastor of the First Congregational Church of Oak Park. Only a few years later, when the Congregational Churches and the Christian Churches merged nationally, he became the chief executive of the new denomination, the Congregational and Christian Churches, with the title of Minister and Secretary of the General Council. Later, when this new short-lived denomination merged with the Evangelical and Reformed Church to form the United Church of Christ, he became Co-President of that national church. At the time of his death, he was a professor at the Chicago Theological Seminary.

Dr. Hoskins' unexpected death required the selection of a

new chairman for the trustees. To take over a position that had been so ably filled by the likes of Baxter, Dunbaugh, and Hoskins would require considerable judgment and diplomacy. Robert Capps, who was vice chairman, was a natural contender, but to avoid certain problems that might have arisen had he been nominated, he removed himself from consideration. After considerable informal discussion among a few leaders, the consensus was that William Clark '40, financial editor of the Chicago *Tribune*, was the best choice. He was selected at the next annual meeting, and no one ever regretted the action.

Institutions of higher learning are no more immune to fads than other human organizations. While for generations groups of colleges had banded together in athletic conferences, for fund raising, and for other special purposes, a new wave of associations were being formed in the sixties. These new organizations, uniting similar institutions, were attempts to improve programs and increase support. In 1966, Illinois College was a founding member of the Mississippi Valley Association. The other members were Culver-Stockton, Elmhurst, Iowa Wesleyan, Lindenwood, North Park, Principia, and Dubuque. An executive director was employed and an office set up in Chicago.

It was hoped that this combined group would be able to secure grants to finance enriching programs and cooperative enterprises. It never worked out. The colleges were too scattered geographically and too diverse to make much of an appeal to fund sources or to carry on programs of significance. After a couple of years, members began to drop out and the whole organization fell apart.

The fifth Fulbright scholarship for overseas study in twelve years was awarded to Richard R. Vuylsteke. The following year a sixth, Henry Clark, received the same honor.

6
A Time of Bewilderment: 1967–1970

The latter years of the decade of the sixties might well be labeled a tragic era in American higher education. Student unrest ebbs and flows on college campuses over the years, but nothing in modern times in America was ever like this distressing period. It started rather mildly in the mid–1960s and had pretty well run its course by 1971. It created havoc on some campuses, while at others, like Illinois College, it was deeply distressing but had little visible effect. I have always been glad that the time for my retirement did not come before the spirit of rebellion subsided. As it was, I saw the College safely through those threatening days and could turn it over to my successor in more normal times.

While many campuses literally were in flames and riots took place in various parts of the nation, there was no disorder at Illinois College. Not a minute of time was lost from classes nor was there any damage done, but it took a great deal of ingenuity and care to ensure that trouble did not break out. Throughout the nation, genuine revolutionaries took advantage of campus unrest and did all they could to fan the flames. The hard-core revolutionaries wanted to do anything to make trouble for the establishment and played up every student dissatisfaction. I recall being in Washington when one of the major demonstrations and marches on the Capitol took place. A mile away, I watched professionals organizing and instructing students in tactics for the march and

the disruption. I do not know who they were, but they were not educators.

A small sample of what was happening across the nation occurred at one of our own commencements during the troubled times. I had been warned by state authorities that Illinois College was slated for a Commencement disruption because its speaker was an industrialist; state agents in plain clothes would be on hand in sufficient numbers to take care of any trouble. Shortly before the procession was to begin, the commander of the state security force asked me to go to a certain part of the audience where about a half-dozen of our students were sitting together and to tell them that if any trouble arose, they would be dealt with severely. I did. The agents then went around with cameras and, at point-blank range and with the full knowledge of the subjects, photographed the outside agitators to let them know that if trouble came, the police would have proof of their presence. The Commencement exercises proceeded without interruption.

It must be remembered that students had some genuine reasons for dissatisfaction. The problems of integration stirred up all sorts of resentment. The Viet Nam War, at first almost totally supported by the American people of all ages, became increasingly unpopular. Then there was the draft, which was a disruptive factor in the lives of young men.

But these were not the basic reason for the trouble, in my opinion. The students were a permissively raised generation, suffering from the theories of Dr. Spock, once the patron saint of parents. The older generation, particularly the parents of students, probably was more to blame than the students themselves. "It was the way they were raised."

My official reports to the trustees for 1965, 1966, and 1967 discussed the situation. Here are excerpts:

1964–65

While this has been another good year for Illinois College, it has been a difficult and demanding one for college administrators

everywhere. Contrary to the expectations of most Americans who had been led to believe that a pot of gold at the end of a rainbow was the answer to all problems, prosperity never before equalled in human history has not resulted in improved human conduct or peace and tranquility. The greater freedom and opportunity for people at all economic and social levels have not resulted in the satisfactions which would seem to follow naturally. There are more agitation, more unrest, and more demonstrations than in times of less affluence and opportunity. Regard for law and authority has been reduced and uncertainty is the order of the day. A college cannot and should not escape its environment. The problems peculiar to our generation plus the vast increase of college age population produces new and difficult demands on educational leadership.

A year later, I wrote as follows:

For many institutions of higher learning, both large and small, 1965–66 has been a year of turmoil and uncertainty. Many colleges have grown too fast for their own good and have not been able to give enough attention to the students they have accepted. This overprivileged generation of young people demands more than is reasonable, but many institutions have not been able to deliver even up to the minimum requirements. The loss of identity as individuals, especially at large universities, and a false understanding of democracy as it relates to college management, together with the special problems of integration and Selective Service have conspired to disturb the peace on far too many campuses of all sizes. I hope and believe that the degree of tranquility so necessary to learning which prevailed here has been due in some measure to the way our students have been treated.

As campus unrest increased nationwide, I included the next few sentences in my 1966–1967 report:

We are having for the most part students from good homes with good standards of behavior and a high degree of responsibility.

Today more than ever before the nominal campus leaders are sometimes opportunists or persons of second level ability.

It seems to me that the colleges that are weathering the cur-

Time of Bewilderment

rent passing storm are those sticking to their ideals and those which are known by students as not being subject to whims of the moment.

Although no part of Illinois College was physically damaged and no classes were interrupted, this does not mean that there were no troubles. There were agitation and many unreasonable demands. These were never met. Rather, we talked and talked and talked.

Students from some of the so-called best homes were often the most difficult. My feelings were more of sadness than dislike for them. Often they seemed to be devoid of reason. I preserved my equilibrium with the knowledge that this was a passing phase for them and for the College, but it was hard. Some of these students were arrogant beyond belief. I recall a freshman in his first semester of college giving me a lecture on how to run the College and pointing out my shortcomings.

Hardest for me to endure was the awareness that reason seemed to have vanished and emotionalism had taken over. I always had believed that logic was an important factor in shaping conduct but here were people to whom logic meant nothing. I saw no reason why students should take out their frustrations over the draft or Viet Nam by rebellion on the campuses of the nation. I used to say that if there was to be a demonstration, it ought to be conducted in front of the post office or some other symbol of the federal government. The College had neither enacted the draft nor started the war.

This is not to say that there were not campus issues to be faced. Disturbed students, whatever the cause of their anxiety, can be counted on to make trouble. Governance—rules and regulations of all sorts—became symbols of oppression to some. They thought that almost everything, except providing for their ease and comfort, should be turned over to the students to run. The one group that was the least anarchistic was the athletes. They understood that direction and teamwork were essential to success.

We had small demands for those things that were fought over on other campuses—open dormitories, student representation on the Board of Trustees and faculty meetings, and the abolition of rules of conduct and requirements for graduation, among others. In the case of proposals that were detrimental to the educational experience and conduct of the College, the only answer was to explain why it was the way it was. We were not going to have open dormitories, students making decisions for which they were not equipped, or conduct that would bring disrespect to the College.

Now, years later, I regard these decisions shared by the administration and the board as among the most important ever made in the history of the College. Since those days we have seen many colleges of our type struggling to regain the approval of constituencies lost by reason of unwise yielding to radicals during that period. The unbroken record of advance and the unfailing reservoir of good will which has sustained the College in its continued progress is in no small measure the result of a firm and sane stand at a time when the easy thing to do would have been to yield to those who made the most noise.

While the unreasonable minority made the headlines and gave whole student bodies a bad name, the more rational majority must bear some of the blame for the events that characterized the era. They did not stand up against what they knew to be wrong; they simply withdrew from the fray. In most places they stopped voting at student elections and let the radicals take over. The result was that student-body officials were no longer properly representative. Ambitious radicals were elected heads of the student governments, and vocal revolutionists took over student newspapers.

While the officers of the student body at Illinois College were, for the most part, rather satisfactory during that period, the same cannot be said for some who presided over *The Rambler* (the student newspaper). I admired the officers of the student association in most of those years, but they

were often harassed and could not operate as well as those who lead in more normal times.

One of the great losses from which colleges and universities have not yet fully recovered was in the field of student publications. In previous generations, a somewhat autocratic but knowledgeable faculty member oversaw the student newspaper and staff members learned the basics of journalism. Then came the revolution. The students did not want to be told anything by anyone. The papers became irresponsible organs of denunciation, not newspapers. Even at Illinois College, I saw issues where reports of athletic contests and major academic events were crowded out by long-winded tirades about alleged crimes against human dignity inflicted on students by heartless and unconcerned administrators. Papers were suspended at many colleges for fear of libel suits as students invoked freedom of the press as their hunting license. Aside from the concern and rage sometimes expressed by parents, alumni, and patrons, the real loss was in learning. The newspaper staff learned little if anything. They could not even be persuaded that grammar and punctuation were "relevant."

Contrary to what might have been thought by some, the tragic era of student unrest proved to be a great triumph for the College. Patrons, alumni, and friends thought more of the College because it withstood, much better than most others, the tests of adversity. The institution weathered the storm for two reasons. First, most of the students had been brought up to be responsible people. Second, the College had the good sense to stick to high standards in spite of those who wanted it to do otherwise.

I was heartened in later years to have almost every one of the handful of leading rebels on this campus during the 1960s come to me after their college days were over and apologize, often in a roundabout way. They now saw things differently and they often expressed appreciation and some admiration for my having stood up to them. I would not want to live

those years over again, but I believe that my conduct at that time ranks among my greatest contributions to the general progress of the College. Although the strain was great on administrators, life went on much as usual on the campus. It was still a time of progress.

In the fall of 1967, the enrollment was the highest in history with 836 students, 55 more than the record of a year before. About 70 were student nurses. New faculty positions had to be filled, and the result was that some 20 new posts had been created in the last decade. New appointees who remained throughout my administration included Dr. Richard Fry, history; Harold Leam, English; and Lynette Seator, Spanish.

The completion of Pixley Hall provided enough new living space that Colonial Inn and Fayerweather House were not needed. Actually, that was the end of the use of Colonial Inn by the College. A few years later it was needed, but the zoning laws had been changed so that it could not be used as a dormitory, and it was subsequently sold.

The Student Center was nearly completed at the opening of classes in 1967 and was dedicated as a Homecoming event. A functional building, it was designed to fit into its special setting and represented an important addition to the campus. I suggested that it should bear the name of one of several people, including President Hudson, the late chairman of the board, Fred Hoskins, or William Jennings Bryan. There was some argument in the board about Bryan because some old timers, who had lived through the political years of the College's most illustrious alumnus, had differed so much with him that they did not want to memorialize him. The matter was postponed and then forgotten. Nothing ever surprised me more than to be told after my retirement that the building was to be named in my honor.

A valuable addition to the program of the College was the opening of a student-operated campus radio station. Its signals could be picked up on a regular radio receiver but only

Time of Bewilderment

The Caine Student Center, built in 1967.

in buildings on the same lighting circuits, for the transmission was over these wires. The moving spirit behind the project was John Clark, a junior from Wilmette. He put the station together and ran it as long as he was in College. Interestingly, his experience provided good training for him; he went into the technical side of radio as his profession. After Clark's graduation, others took over. From time to time the station would close down for a semester or a year for lack of student interest but someone would always come along and put it back into business. It provided experience for a substantial number of students and was a considerable benefit to their education.

Cooperation with MacMurray College was a perennial topic of discussion. As previously indicated, Illinois College students took music courses at MacMurray, and there was a joint band. When both colleges came upon difficult times in the early 1950s, the trustees of both institutions seriously discussed closer and more extensive joint ventures. The possibility of an alleged merger so inflamed some of the Illinois

College people that all further discussions ended in 1954–1955 and President Selden, an advocate of closer cooperation, resigned. The opening of MacMurray's new College for Men aggravated the friction between the two institutions, and ten years elapsed before there was any prospect of new cooperative ventures.

In the college year 1967–1968, Illinois College proposed a teaching plan in foreign languages that it thought would be beneficial to all. Both colleges taught French, Spanish, and German. French was the most popular, and there were sufficient students at both colleges to make good-sized advanced classes. Not so in Spanish and German. While there were

Honorary degree recipients flank President Caine at the 1967 Commencement. *From far left:* Senator Everett Dirksen, the Commencement speaker; President Emeritus H. Gary Hudson (1937–1953); J. Cordell Moore '36, assistant secretary of the U.S. Department of Interior; President Caine; Rufus Z. Smith '44, director of Canadian Affairs for the U.S. State department; and former faculty member Robert L. Scranton, professor of classical art and archaeology, University of Chicago.

Time of Bewilderment

enough first year students in each at both colleges, advanced classes were so small as to be uneconomical. It was proposed that advanced classes in one language be offered on one of the campuses and in the other language on the other. MacMurray rejected the plan. The only thing that was agreed upon was a schedule of commencement dates so that the two graduations would be held on successive weekends. This arrangement held for the rest of my administration and was much appreciated by the community.

Ending also was the only genuine academic cooperation in effect at that time. As previously discussed, Illinois College had entered into an extensive program of using Asian scholars brought to the United States by foundations and the State Department. The program cost the College a modest $6500 per year. MacMurray paid us $2500 and had the use of half the time of the scholars but withdrew from the program on the grounds that its interests were more in the Middle East.

In talking with an alumnus in government service, I learned of a program offered by the State Department that could bring an added dimension to our emphasis on foreign affairs. Each year, the State Department brought back from abroad some of its employees to keep them in touch with the affairs at home. They used their returnees to interpret the work of our representatives overseas to the public. To accomplish both purposes, a limited number of teams of Foreign Service officers were available to spend a week in scattered communities where their services could be used to advantage.

I went to Washington and found that there were fewer than a dozen such teams, which were to be sent to places where they would have maximum exposure. I offered to take one of the teams and schedule them in communities in Illinois and Missouri for as many appearances as they could handle. A team was assigned to us with Illinois College as their headquarters. So successful were our efforts that for three consecutive years we were able to get such a group. At the end of

that time it was decided that this part of the country had had more than its share of attention and that teams would have to go elsewhere.

Each set of visitors was composed of five people, including a coordinating officer who lived in Washington. The other members had been stationed in different foreign posts and had different fields of expertise. One might be an economist, another an agricultural expert, and another a military attaché. All were college graduates, some with advanced degrees. To our surprise, the first team was headed by Rufus Z. Smith, an expert on Canadian affairs who had graduated from Illinois College in 1944.

Not only did all of these people lead classes and convocations at Illinois College and MacMurray but they spoke to service clubs, women's organizations, and almost every other kind of gathering here and in communities for miles around. We also arranged for the teams to go for a day to other college communities in this area for similar appointments. It was a most stimulating and informational program.

It was the sesquicentennial year for the state of Illinois and there were to be activities in celebration in each county. Morgan County inaugurated its activities with exercises in Beecher Hall, the state's oldest college building, and in historic Smith House on the College campus.

One of the recurring activities of the area which brought hundreds of high-school students to the campus was the Southwestern District Illinois Junior Academy of Science Fair. Some 300 exhibits of high-school students would be set up in Memorial Gymnasium, and more than 100 judges would decide the winners in the various categories. Top winners went on to the finals of the state competition. The science fair was held every spring at Illinois College for many years.

Students are not always intent on traditional learning. After it was learned that a student at McKendree College had eaten fifty-three hard-boiled eggs in an hour, an Illinois Col-

lege student, before fifty-five spectators, ate forty-five in that amount of time in a vain attempt at superiority.

State and federal funds to assist students in paying for college expenses continued to expand. By 1967, students at Illinois College were receiving more than half a million dollars. Like so many other government grant programs, the politically attractive thing to do is to liberalize requirements. For many years a burning question at meetings of the Association of American Colleges had to do with whether or not independent institutions of higher learning should receive direct grants from the government. Until that year, a dwindling majority had always opposed it as a danger to their independence or as a violation of the separation of church and state on the part of the majority (which were church related). That year, the association not only voted to take such money but actively campaigned for public funds. I was in the minority that voted against the plan.

Financially, the College was doing amazingly well. We had enough money in the building fund that only a modest effort sufficed to obtain the funds needed to build the Student Center. The College also had restored to the endowment fund all the money that had been borrowed for current operations in the previous administrations and was able to transfer $350,000 from gifts to the endowment.

Several significant gifts were received during the year. The will of Mrs. Robert Frackelton, whose husband was a member of the Class of 1888 and a leading Cleveland industrialist, left $100,000 to the College in his memory. Elzie Weber '09 left a similar amount that came to the College at about the same time. Quite a number of other bequests of lesser size were being received every year. All went into the endowment, which was increasing at a good pace. Over the past seven years, bequests increased the endowment by more than $700,000.

Dr. Eleanor Miller, professor of psychology, retired after thirty-seven years of teaching. Only Dr. Julian M. Sturtevant,

the first teacher and second president, and Dr. Samuel Adams, who taught science courses, served the College as a faculty and staff member longer than she. Sturtevant's term was fifty-six years and Adams's forty years. The quality of Dr. Miller's contribution to the work of the College was as noteworthy as the length of service.

In a year when institutional practices of all sorts were under heavy attack by young people everywhere, required chapel and convocation became a focal point for restless students. Required chapel had never been popular with all students, but it had existed since the opening of the College in 1829. Chapel was in earlier years a hodgepodge of all sorts of meetings, some of which had little to do with religion. During my first year, the trustees had accepted my recommendation and added a required convocation so that the secular and the sacred would be taken care of separately.

Until a short time before, one of the requirements for being listed and supported by the Presbyterian Church was to have required chapel. This regulation had been abolished under the pressure of student unrest, although many church colleges still maintained the requirement. Convocations served an additional role as a special opportunity to foster a sense of community, to present topics of general interest, and to provide a common educational experience. It was no longer a question of whether these exercises, both religious and otherwise, were a worthy part of the College program; rather, it became a question of whether they could be maintained effectively in the face of mounting student independence.

The matter came before the board in its 1968 meeting and evoked considerable discussion. It was decided that these programs were valuable and no change should be made, although it was recognized that some changes might be necessary in the near future. At the next annual meeting, the matter came up again because of the growing opposition on the campus, including some from the faculty. Chapel was

presented as "forced worship." If it were that, it had been so for some 140 years and it could be rightfully maintained that when a student enrolled at an institution knowing that chapel was required, he or she made the choice to conform. The trustees asked the faculty to study the question and the matter was taken up at the 1970 annual meeting. Chapel, as generations had known it, was in its last year. At the 1970 meeting, after more discussion, the board affirmed the weekly convocation requirement but made chapel voluntary. As such, it ceased to be a potent force in the College.

The College suffered a serious loss when its vice chairman, Robert Capps '17, was killed in an automobile accident. He had been a trustee for twenty-two years.

A noteworthy large class of new trustees was elected without term to fill accumulated vacancies. One was Robert W. Reneker, chief executive officer and chairman of the board of Swift and Company, whose son and daughter-in-law were alumni. He resigned a few years later when he was elected president of the board of the Boy Scouts of America. The three others were alumni: Robert F. Sibert '36, president of the New Method Book Bindery; Frances McReynolds Smith '33, of the Center of Pacific Studies of the University of California at Santa Cruz; William Wilton '39, president of the Jasper Blackburn Corporation; and Dr. Ray Carlton Jones, pastor of the Bryn Mawr Community Church of Chicago.

Every year since the summer of 1955, renovation and new construction had been taking place on the campus. Old Whipple Hall, which had been empty since Crispin Science Hall was finished, was renovated in the summer of 1968 to provide headquarters for the Education Department, Placement, Student Aid, and Admissions.

A newcomer to the faculty was William Horton, whose father had retired after long service as professor of physics. The younger Horton taught mathematics.

A new program was also inaugurated that fall. The College became a member of the Affiliated Artists Program, which

The trustees of Illinois College, 1968–1969. *Front row from the left:* William E. Wilton, Arthur J. French, C. Ellsworth Black, William N. Clark, L. Vernon Caine, Robert R. Hartman. *Row 2:* Jack R. Hartong, Paul Findley, Emily H. Eppenger, Dorothy Van Rosendal, Robert J. Wood, F. Osborne Elliott. *Row 3:* Arthur C. Hart, Ray Carlton Jones, Robert F. Sibert, Richard H. Ewert, Lyndle W. Hess, F. Harris Rowe. *Row 4:* D. O. Milligan, Robert W. Reneker, Walter R. Bellatti, Robert B. Oxtoby. *Not pictured:* Richard H. Wayne, Harry J. Dunbaugh, Harold R. Martin.

sought to give promising young musicians and artists an opportunity to work. With most of the costs covered by grants, an artist in residence was based on the campus for a year at a time to perform throughout the area.

Illinois College's first artist was John Walker, a graduate of Jacksonville High School and a former student at Illinois College. He was a very popular vocalist. During the year, in addition to singing on the campus on many occasions, he gave concerts in the surrounding area. The program contin-

ued for several years with other artists assigned for one-year periods.

One of many special programs during the year was a chapel program led by three former military chaplains. At this time, the rightness of the war in Viet Nam was a topic of vigorous discussion, and many students had grave doubts about the morality of a minister participating in a military organization.

One of the greatest surprises of my days at Illinois College occurred when an article in our little house organ, *Comments*, attracted national attention. I wrote the piece for the small quarterly publication, which went out to parents and friends of the College. The lead article was "Who Runs the College?" (see Appendix B). I wrote it out of deep concern over widespread demand by students throughout the nation to have a major voice in setting college policies. Not only did I receive scores of commendatory letters but the article itself was reprinted in publications all over the country, including the *Congressional Record*. It appeared in trade journals, on the editorial pages of newspapers, and in church and educational publications. We had more demands for copies than we could supply. One of the results was an invitation from the Illinois Chamber of Commerce to speak to their educational advisory committee. The Chamber also reprinted the article.

About the same time, possibly because of the article, television station KHQA of Quincy asked me to come over for a half-hour interview on student unrest in the colleges and what to do about it. As a result of the interview, I received a great deal of mail. While just about all of it was in praise of my convictions, the most laudatory included a check for $1,000 for the College. An industrialist who had heard the broadcast said he wanted to support a college that took that view of things. That was only the first of many yearly contributions from him.

From time to time, in order to manage the College most

effectively, we called on outsiders to take a look at various phases of the College operation. The Association of American Colleges, of which we were a member, had instituted a program of supplying newly retired outstanding college administrators to make inspections of colleges at a modest cost. Dr. Theodore A. Distler, former dean of LaFayette College and president of Franklin and Marshall, who had just retired as president of the association, visited us under that program. While he investigated most aspects of management, he focused particularly on the academic program and especially on a proposal under study by the faculty for an interdepartmental program for freshmen and seniors. His visit had some impact on a program the College adopted a year later. We also arranged with the president of MacMurray College to confer with Dr. Distler about the possibility of certain cooperative efforts between the two colleges.

A unique event of considerable educational and public relations value was the Model Illinois Constitutional Convention in April 1969. The idea of Elizabeth Zeigler, who taught political science, this student gathering was held in anticipation of the actual state convention that was to write a new constitution. Twenty-four colleges and universities in Illinois sent 116 delegates to the gathering. Among the speakers were Lieutenant Governor Paul Simon and U.S. Senator Charles Percy. The model constitution prepared by the students was delivered to Governor Richard Ogilvie, and copies were sent to various other state officials.

Earlier, at the inauguration of a new president at another college, I had made the acquaintance of Dr. Paul Chung, a dentist who was a member of the faculty of Northwestern University and formerly the Korean consul in Chicago. He asked me to have lunch with him when I came to Chicago, and from our conversations came the idea of inviting the Korean ambassador, Dong Jo Kim, to visit the College for a couple of days as one of our distinguished visitors. He made

arrangements for me to visit the Ambassador the next time I was in Washington. Thus began a memorable chain of events.

Ambassador Kim, who had a doctorate from Harvard University, was glad to accept an invitation to come to Illinois College and to participate in everything we could arrange. He was a good speaker and was well received as he addressed a convocation and a joint service club luncheon. The ambassador also led discussions in a couple of classes and was interviewed by the press and radio. He spoke of the economic condition of Korea, the need for American aid and military assistance in holding off the forces of Communism, and of the recent *Pueblo* incident in which North Korea captured an American ship. He enjoyed a well-attended reception and made a most favorable impression. A feature of his visit was a private meeting with sixteen Korean nationals, mostly of academic orientation, from as far away as Champaign and Chicago.

We invited Ambassador Kim to return at Commencement and awarded him an honorary doctor of laws degree. He was profuse in his thanks and in his distribution of gifts. But that was not the end of the story. He invited me to have lunch with him at the embassy the next time I was in Washington. The other guests were the honorary Korean consul of New Orleans and his wife. He was an American businessman who did the honors for Korea in the absence of an official representative in that city. Mrs. Kim and two young men of the embassy staff also shared the occasion. Each place was set with sterling silver, including chopsticks of the same material. I sat by Mrs. Kim, who told me what was in the various Korean dishes and who gave me a lesson in eating with chopsticks. I gave that up as too slow and resorted to the knife, fork, and spoon. The conversation was delightful.

On the way into the dining room, we had passed through a room containing some large cabinets in which were displayed wonderful Korean vases of ancient origin. The ambas-

sador explained that these art treasures could no longer be shipped out of Korea but added that "An ambassador [could] get them." When the meal was over, we again passed through that room. He said to the man from New Orleans and to me, "You like those vases, don't you? Take one." We protested that we could not think of doing so; they were too valuable. He insisted and finally each of us chose one. He then said, "Take another." We protested vigorously but finally we each chose another one. He sent a servant out for some beautiful boxes in which the vases were wrapped for safe transportation. I carried mine onto the plane on my return flight. One was 800 years old.

We were to have an alumni meeting in Washington, and it occurred to me that the ambassador would be quite an attraction as a speaker for that group. He readily responded to my invitation and made a good speech at the dinner. On our way back after the meeting, he asked me what I was doing the next night. He explained that he was giving a reception for a group of bankers and top financial officials of Korea who were visiting the United States. He would like to have me come as a guest. I accepted his invitation.

The embassy, with its beautiful garden in the rear, was the site of the reception, which included about 100 people (more than half of them Americans). There were more generals than I had ever seen at one time, and many government officials from both the executive and legislative branches—especially those that had to do with Korean matters. Among the American officials I met there was Arthur Burns, chairman of the Federal Reserve Board. Words fail me when it comes to describing the food. There was hot and cold Korean and American food in profusion. I was particularly impressed by a great piece of driftwood festooned with strawberries as big as apricots on toothpicks, to be dipped in powdered sugar. It was a gala occasion.

A few years later, a scandal broke out in Washington. The charge was made that Korean officials had been bribing mem-

Time of Bewilderment

bers of Congress to vote in favor of legislation beneficial to their country. It appeared that the key person in the action was Ambassador Dong Jo Kim. When he was about to be asked to testify concerning these doings, he returned to Korea and was appointed a member of the president's cabinet. All efforts to get him back to testify failed. While it appeared that he was engaged in practices on behalf of his nation that were contrary to American law, from his standpoint he was no villain. Whatever the facts of the matter, I knew him to be a high-minded, very intelligent, and deeply interesting person who made a real contribution to education at Illinois College and provided some memorable times for me. I wish I could talk to him again.

Two of the alumni of Illinois College were appointed in 1968 by the newly elected governor, James Thompson, to positions in his cabinet. Ray Dickerson '29, a Champaign contractor who had built the new University of Illinois field house, was named to head the Department of Business and Economic Development, and William Cellini '58 was appointed director of the Department of Public Works and Buildings. The College honored them with a reception at the president's home.

Slater Food Service rounded out a full decade of service at Baxter Hall. As a token of appreciation, its officers arranged for the ARA Historic Foundation to send its collection of original Civil War documents for exhibition.

One of the most unpleasant incidents in my administration took place that year. A local group of investors had built a television station in Jacksonville, a venture that proved to be a failure. Unbeknown to college officials, they employed three faculty members as news and weather men on daily broadcasts. The situation was not to be tolerated. These faculty members had to devote major blocks of time to their television programs when it interfered not with classes but with other normal faculty duties. Their mistake was, as I saw it and informed them, that they had taken substantial em-

ployment that interfered with their duties and diverted their attention from College responsibilities, and they had done so without consulting with any college administrator. They claimed that aside from classes, their time was their own to do with as they pleased. I told them that they must give up their employment at the station or I would ask the board to terminate their appointments at the College for the next year.

One of the three hid a tape recorder in his clothing and came into my office. His plan was to anger me so that I would make statements that would reflect adversely on me. While he succeeded in the former, he did not have much luck in the latter. He took the tapes to the chairman of the Faculty Committee of the board, but after the chairman had heard a little of them and understood what was going on, he declined to listen or to talk further unless the faculty member agreed to have me present. That ended the matter.

The board's action subsequently required the three either to give up their work at the station or to resign from the faculty. One chose to resign; a second was dismissed for this and other reasons; and the third gave up his television career and resumed his normal teaching duties without any unpleasantness. The trustees then adopted regulations that required permission from the president before a faculty member could accept any substantial ongoing extra employment during the academic year.

Charles Martin of White Hall, an all-time great basketball player, ended a record-breaking career that rivaled anything in the annals of the College. He tied the record set by Bill Shouse in 1949 by scoring 535 points and was selected for the Conference All-Star and NAIA District 20 teams. His career record of 1510 points was a new high. He had 25 rebounds in one game and a season record of 405.

During the second semester, for the first time in the history of the College, enrollment was closed for the fall term because capacity had been reached.

One of the major figures in the history of Illinois College

in his era, Harry Dunbaugh, died that year. A trustee for forty-six years and a former chairman of the board as well as one of the leading lawyers of Chicago and a major benefactor of the College, he was remembered in a way most helpful to the faculty. The income from a fund subscribed in his memory, increased over succeeding years by his widow, was awarded to the full-time teacher who was judged to have done the best job for the year. In addition to a trophy and having his or her name inscribed on a plaque, the honoree received a monetary award that later grew to be $1,000.

Commencement in 1969 was more historic than usual because the great-grandson of Julian M. Sturtevant, a member of the Yale Band and second president of the College, was the speaker. Dr. Julian Munson Sturtevant, professor of chemistry and molecular biology at Yale University, was the honored guest.

One of the most incredible developments of recent years has been inflation. When I came to Illinois College, the highest paid professor received $4,500 per year and the president's salary was far below that of the newest instructor today. It cost less than $500,000 to run the entire institution for a year, and it was not until 1969 that the annual budget showed expenditures of over $1 million. At my retirement in 1973, the amount was just under $2 million. Almost all the increase was attributable to growth in enrollment and improvement in the real earnings of all the employees. Inflation was only just beginning to make a difference. I recall how hard it was to believe, in 1969, that Illinois College's operations cost a million dollars.

The growth of the College included healthy growth of the endowment. In 1969, Kenneth Danskin '29 and his wife Katharine gave $100,000 to endow the system of sabbatical leaves for faculty members. Previously, the cost of semester leaves for study, travel, and research at full pay had had to come from the current budget. Now the income from this new endowment was available for that purpose. Kenneth, a

Jacksonville resident in his early days, was a chemist and had worked for oil companies in Texas and out of the London office of a British corporation. He was given the alumnus Distinguished Service Citation at Commencement.

The College added two city blocks east of the football field to the campus. The eight-acre addition brought the entire campus to sixty-three acres. While there was no actual need for more land, the opportunity to acquire it was so advantageous that it could not be passed over.

Many years before, this area had been the site of the Harris family home. The land became the inheritance of five sisters, one of whom had just died, and it was now necessary to settle the estate. Mrs. Ruth Bohan of Kansas City, Missouri, one of the sisters and the widow of a physician on the faculty of the University of Kansas Medical School, was in charge. The family did not want to see the property developed for housing. Mrs. Bohan offered to give the College her fifth and another sister would give half of her share. Thus, three-tenths was a gift. The College purchased the remainder. Mrs. Bohan also paid for the establishment of a memorial that consisted of a plaque and a bench with plantings about it. The College seeded the land in grass, and it became a play area for summer sports in the community.

When I went to Kansas City to work out the arrangement, Mrs. Bohan put me up in a downtown club and invited me to a dinner at the Art Institute. It was a special celebration with the curator of the Boston Museum as speaker.

By the opening of college in the fall of 1969, student unrest was ebbing all across the nation. It had come on gradually, and it abated in the same manner. Anxious administrators discussed whether this was a lull or if the worst was yet to come. It turned out that disorder had been a transient phenomenon that would be followed by tranquility.

The fall term opened with an enrollment of 920, the largest in the history of the College up to that time, or since. Five years before, the count had been 642 and ten years before,

464. There was a slight decline the following year. That slight downward trend continued for a time. It is noteworthy that at the peak of enrollment for the nation, the American Council on Education reported that the capacity of educational institutions was 15 percent more than the enrollment. In true American fashion, we had built too much. Not so at Illinois College.

The College experienced a new high in congressional representation. Ralph Smith '37, Speaker of the Illinois General Assembly, was appointed to fill the Senate seat made vacant by the death of U.S. Senator Everett Dirksen. In the House of Representatives were Paul Findley '45 and Charlotte Reid '34.

Now, at last, after years of shortage, graduate schools were

Reception for Ralph Smith '37, newly elected Speaker of the Illinois General Assembly. He is being congratulated by Hugh Green '09, former Speaker. *From the left:* Mrs. Smith, Ralph Smith, Elizabeth Caine, Hugh Green, President Caine, Harris Rowe '47, member of the General Assembly Thomas Rose.

turning out more than enough Ph.D.s to meet the demand for college teachers. Along with the easing of student tension, the search for good teachers became much easier. The Illinois College faculty showed their vitality and zeal for learning. The previous summer, ten faculty members had been abroad and two others engaged in summer study with the aid of National Science Foundation grants.

For some two years, under the leadership of Dean Yeager, the faculty had been discussing the pros and cons of the adoption of a new required course for freshmen. It would be interdisciplinary in nature and equivalent to about one-fifth of the work of the year. The committee charged with developing the proposal presented it to the faculty, and, in the end, it was adopted by about a 2-to-1 vote. The faculty was by no means unanimous in their support.

As set up for the following year, the program was called "Man in Change." The focus was on humankind's changing conception of itself and dealt with environment, communication, and social patterns. It drew on all the social sciences, the arts, science, and religion as well as other branches of knowledge. Six faculty members from different departments constituted the staff. Material was often presented in large lecture sections with the group then breaking into smaller seminars where discussions took place. Over the years, the content of the course changed considerably.

This program was never fully popular with students, and some departments never accepted it as the best way to use students' time. Often, it was difficult to induce certain needed faculty members to participate. Some professors thought that their knowledge in areas beyond their department was not adequate for them to be leading discussions. Although the course was offered for a decade, there was always a current of dissatisfaction in the faculty; it was finally dropped from the curriculum.

One of the interesting fringe benefits of being a president is being invited in a sort of ex officio capacity to many events.

In the fall of 1969, the refurbished Lovejoy Monument in Alton was rededicated. Illinois College's first president, Edward Beecher, had been a close associate of Elijah P. Lovejoy, the antislavery editor who was killed when his press was destroyed by proslavery partisans. Beecher had come back to Jacksonville the afternoon before Lovejoy was murdered.

Although I thought it would be better to postpone it until my retirement, the trustees insisted that I have my portrait painted. The artist selected was Shirley Friend, a Chicagoan who had painted portraits for a number of the first families of that city. The artist came down to get a feeling for the campus, to see where the portrait was to be hung, and to obtain more information about me. In addition to depicting educational leadership on a wooded campus, she decided to show that I had also been a builder. The background of the portrait contains trees and Rammelkamp Chapel.

I made several trips to Chicago to sit in Miss Friend's studio and I was surprised to find that it was more tiring than I supposed. The artist brought the nearly finished painting to Jacksonville to touch up; she even made a few slight alterations at Elizabeth's suggestion. There was a fine reception at the unveiling, attended by community and college people. The portrait now hangs in the Faculty-Trustee Room along with oil paintings of other presidents of long service. To complete the collection, we secured enlarged photographs of the other presidents as well.

For the second time in my administration, Illinois College was host to the governor of Illinois. Richard B. Ogilvie accepted an invitation to speak at a morning convocation and to have lunch at our home.

With the knowledge that the College would be celebrating its sesquicentennial in 1979, the Board of Trustees authorized the appointment of a committee to outline the direction the College should take. Since 1958, it had been progressing according to the Forward Step Plan, now nearly completed. The new committee was to chart the future beyond that blueprint.

Shirley Friend chats with Chairman of the Board William Clark '40 at the unveiling ceremonies for her portrait of President Caine.

Lyndle Hess, a leading member of the board, was named chairman. The committee was to seek information from all segments of the College family and to consider program, facilities, financing, and the objectives of the institution for the years ahead.

Another State Department team came to Illinois College and fanned out to schools and organizations all over the area. This one was headed by the deputy director of the Office of Soviet Union Affairs and was composed of experts on Latin America, the Middle East, and East Asia.

In March 1968, a committee of outside educational experts issued its report entitled "Strengthening Higher Education in Illinois." The governor had appointed this prestigious commission to explore ways in which the state might help the private colleges of Illinois. Aside from more scholarship

money for students, the commission proposed direct aid to the institutions themselves. This report became the basis for increased activity with the General Assembly. Because Jacksonville was near Springfield, I was called upon to do considerable lobbying when measures relating to the welfare of private colleges and universities received legislative attention. I had previously done some lobbying in North Dakota and Minnesota. While it was an interesting experience, it did not increase my respect for the legislative process.

The chief arguments for public aid to private colleges were two. First, private sector graduates made great contributions to the general welfare in every field of endeavor. Second, by educating large numbers of students in private colleges at no cost to the taxpayers, these institutions had reduced the cost of public education very greatly.

Private colleges had previously succeeded in their efforts to get student aid for college costs from the state to help make up the differential between tuition costs at the private and public institutions. Now we were successful in getting funds paid directly to the private colleges and universities to help educate every in-state student who attended.

Earlier, we discovered that ambassadors welcomed the opportunity to speak on behalf of their nations here in the Midwest, so we invited several more during the next three years. Our congressman and Illinois College trustee, Paul Findley, spent some time on the campus each year. He spoke to at least one convocation and led class discussions. Aside from the important contributions to learning as a participant in college classes and discussions, he opened the way for many important visitors to the campus. The Commencement speaker in 1970 was an example.

Congressman Findley arranged for me to meet with Rolf Pauls, the ambassador from West Germany, to ask him to be the Commencement speaker. I went to the German embassy, a new building of modern design, in the woods of Virginia just outside of Washington. We stood in the window on the

third floor and looked out over the parking lot. All the employees' cars were of German make, and he said, "It looks like a Volkswagen dealer's parking lot."

The ambassador was a guest at the alumni luncheon before the Commencement exercises and was greatly interested in what went on. An officer in World War II, he had been wounded and lost an arm. We assigned a student to assist him. He took down her name and address and sent her a handsome present. The ambassador made a good speech and received an honorary doctor of laws degree. Not only did he refuse an honorarium, but he made a gift of $1,000 to the College. He also presented me with a beautifully bound and inscribed volume of Goethe's *Italian Journey*.

That Commencement had some other noteworthy features. For the only time in the eighteen commencements of my administration, one speaker did not make it. President Robert Fauth of Eden Theological Seminary came down with appendicitis and Dean Walter Bruggeman had to take his place as the baccalaureate speaker.

For the second time in my days as president, an alumnus came back for his seventy-fifth anniversary. He was Dr. William Garrett, professor emeritus of mathematics at Baker University.

The group receiving honorary degrees is also worthy of note. They included not only the ambassador but also Colonel Kenneth Crawford '51, commandant of the Judge Advocate General's School; William Findley '36, professor of engineering at Brown University; Edward Johnston '39, former lieutenant governor of Hawaii and now high commissioner of the Trust Territories of the Pacific; and Ralph Smith '37, newly appointed U.S. senator and former Speaker of the Illinois General Assembly.

7
The End of an Era:
1970–1973

For the second time during my administration, there was a change in the deanship. Dean Yeager, who had done an excellent job for twelve years, decided that he would rather be a full-time professor than an administrator. He was, at heart, a teacher; he also wanted more time to write. Much as I regretted his decision, I respected his wishes. With considerable reluctance, I had set in motion the year before the process of selecting his successor.

Since the position is that of leadership of the faculty, it was important that faculty members should play an important role in selecting the new dean. A committee with representation from each division of the faculty was constituted, and the search was underway. From a long list of prospects and a small number of very promising people, the unanimous choice was Dr. Wallace N. Jamison, who had served as president of the New Brunswick Theological Seminary in New Jersey.

Dr. Jamison was born in Egypt of Presbyterian missionary parents. His A.B. degree was from Westminster College in Pennsylvania. He earned a Th.B. degree from Princeton Seminary and a Ph.D. in history from the University of Edinburgh, Scotland. An ordained minister, he had served as a chaplain in World War II and as chairman of the history department at Westminster College. With a keen mind, a breadth of interests, a wealth of experience and travel, and a superior liberal arts education, he was by far the strongest

candidate. His speaking and singing abilities and his flair for leadership enhanced his value to the College and community.

Dr. Yeager returned to full-time teaching and, upon the retirement of Dr. Malcolm Stewart, became the chairman of the Department of Philosophy and Religion. He continued to exercise vigorous leadership in the affairs of the College, and, like his predecessor, Dr. Hildner, who had followed the same course, he did not interfere with the work of the new dean.

The first three years of the decade of the seventies, the end of my administration, were good years. The tensions of the days of student unrest subsided, and the campus became more normal. Because I was ending my era of leadership was no reason to delay or curtail plans for the future of the College. I would be the tenth president to pass from the scene, but the College would continue. The long-range planning committee was at work and a new library was being planned.

As the days of student unrest receded, I could not keep from thinking of the enormous changes that had taken place in the financing of a college education and of attitudes concerning it. The evolution took place in about a decade. In 1960, except for some vestiges of the GI Bill, no student aid from tax sources was available. Ten years later, Illinois College students were the beneficiaries of more than $800,000, and the amount would be more than $1 million before I retired. Many students were still employed, both on and off campus, but it was nothing like it used to be. It was a happier day for the colleges because they no longer had to scratch for student-aid money and carry student accounts, some of which were never paid.

While I favored the aid, although it was sometimes excessive, I regretted the change in attitude. In the early days of government grants, many were reluctant to take the help because it smacked of charity. By 1970, aid was regarded as an entitlement, and most people were out to get their full share. This attitude reached into other kinds of federal programs. It is a major reason for the distressing financial condition of

our government and for some of the decline in the moral fiber of the nation.

In the fall of 1970, the enrollment of women outstripped the housing space of the previous year, and Fayerweather House was reopened. In keeping with the idea of giving students more responsibility for their own lives, it became an honor dormitory. The mature students assigned to live there ran the place themselves without a resident director. It worked out very well.

A grant from the National Endowment for the Humanities, the Xerox Corporation, and the National Gallery of Art provided a special educational opportunity for the College and the community: the showing of the thirteen-part "Civilisation" film series, later released for television presentation. This series, narrated by Kenneth Clark and produced by the British Broadcasting Company, was a motion-picture history of the cultural achievements that shaped Western man: his art, his architecture, his philosophy, and his technical achievements. So many townspeople and students wanted to see it that four showings of each weekly episode were necessary.

A noteworthy event was the visit of Dr. Ashraf Ghorbal and his wife. He was ambassador from the United Arab Republic (Egypt), but at the time of his visit the Egyptians had not yet restored diplomatic relations with the United States. Relations had been broken off when President Eisenhower had sent American marines into Lebanon to forestall a Mideast war over the Suez Canal. Consequently, Dr. Ghorbal was working through the Indian embassy. He said he carried out his usual duties, but the fiction was that Egypt communicated through India's representative. Relations were restored soon after his visit, and he was again ambassador.

Dr. Ghorbal was delighted to have the opportunity to visit us and to be able to speak in the Midwest about his nation's side of the Israel-Arab controversy. He attributed his lack of invitations to speak to Jewish opposition. He was an able

and genial representative of his nation and an excellent speaker.

I corresponded with him at later times and often saw him on television. When Arab terrorists held a group of Americans hostage in a downtown Washington hotel, he went in and persuaded them to free the captives. He was always at President Sadat's side when the Camp David conference was seen on television, and he was the host of the three American presidents when they flew to Cairo to Sadat's funeral.

Two noteworthy retirements took place. At the end of the year, Charles Barlow '29, who since 1962 had headed the Education Department, ended his academic career. He had also been employed by the College in the 1930s.

Dr. C. Ellsworth Black, a trustee for twenty-four years and vice chairman of the board, concluded a tenure that spanned the history of the College. He had succeeded his father, Dr. Carl E. Black, who had become a trustee in 1900. The Blacks were descendants of William Kirby, a member of the Yale Band.

Illinois College produced more than its share of lawyers, and many went on to positions of considerable responsibility. That year, Charles J. Ryan '47 became a judge of the Central Illinois Circuit, joining three other alumni there: Paul C. Verticchio '38, Gail E. McWard '39, and Richard Mills '51.

At a time when college enrollment was beginning to level off and in some liberal arts colleges actually declining, Illinois College was operating at near capacity. It had its highest second semester ever in 1971. These were good students: entering freshmen scored 25 percent above the national average.

Three faculty members were granted semester leaves at full pay, and another earned a National Endowment for the Humanities Fellowship for a year of study in Europe.

This turned out to be the final year of teaching for two of the most capable members of the faculty. Dr. Seybold, co-chairman of the English Department, had been on the faculty

End of an Era

The Class of 1970 and their Commencement guests.

since 1946. She suffered a stroke and had to give up teaching. To qualify for full retirement benefits, she was given a leave of absence until 1975, when she would reach the normal retirement age. She had served her alma mater faithfully and well.

Dr. Hildner, chairman of the History Department and dean of the College from 1938 to 1958, turned sixty-eight and retired. Few members of the faculty in the long history of the College made a greater contribution, not only to the College but to the church and community.

Illinois College would be 150 years old at the end of the decade, and plans for the celebration were being made. They included a financial campaign, with part of the money to be raised designated for the construction of a new library. A

committee made up of various segments of the College drew up the specifications for the library, and plans were completed during 1972. Money was being raised for the Sesquicentennial Fund all the while.

These years were rich in special educational opportunities from outside the campus. For the second successive year, a State Department five-person team spent a week working out of Illinois College. They spread out to a number of neighboring colleges, including some in Missouri. Since they were experts on China and the Soviet Union, these teams were a special attraction for many outside the College.

No less important and interesting was a team from the National Endowment for the Humanities under the auspices of the Woodrow Wilson Foundation. Their theme was "A Sense of Place." They stressed local and family history, folk music, and the need for people to "belong" and to appreciate their heritage and environment. It was an appealing and significantly humane emphasis.

An event of a quite different nature created quite a stir in the educational community of the entire area. Not long before, our astronauts had for the first time walked on the moon. They returned safely, bringing with them rocks from the moon's crust. The moon rocks were incorporated into a special exhibit. Having heard about the exhibit, I contacted the National Aeronautics and Space Administration and put in a bid for the exhibit to be displayed at Illinois College. I was told that the moon rocks could not be shipped but must be personally carried to the place where they were to be shown. I replied that I was to be in Washington in a short time and would personally bring them back to Jacksonville. The agency agreed to let us have them for a week but told me that they could not be checked as baggage on a plane; they would have to be hand carried. I agreed to NASA's terms.

One of my sons was on the faculty at DePauw University at that time, so Elizabeth and I drove over to Greencastle where she visited while I took a plane from Indianapolis to

End of an Era

Washington. I picked up the strangely shaped exhibit that included the rocks and received written instructions to turn it over to a person who would come from Chicago in a week to carry it there for a showing; he would have certain identification that I should check.

My strange carry-on baggage attracted considerable attention in the airport, and I had to explain to the airline what I had and get permission to board the plane before the rest of the passengers. When I got back to DePauw University, my son informed me that some of the science faculty there were anxious to see the moon rocks. So the first informal showing was held at DePauw.

The display at Crispin Science Hall had been well publicized and attracted thousands of people. Schools from all the area surrounding Jacksonville bused their students in at specified times, and older people from miles around came to see the moon rocks.

Those who frequented the campus in the spring of 1971 were not likely to forget the emergence of a hoard of seventeen-year locusts. Live insects covered the trees, and the dead ones covered the ground. They had to be raked up and disposed of before Commencement. One had to see them to believe the extent of the infestation. They reminded me of the grasshoppers in the Dakotas during the Dust Bowl years of the thirties. If they are in a seventeen-year cycle, the College cannot look forward to the spring of 1988 with pleasure.

A great deal of interest was created when Northwestern University began its historic digs at the Koster site not far from Jacksonville and uncovered layer after layer of civilizations that had occupied the area over the centuries. Professor Stuart Struever, who was in charge of the project, was a speaker at the College.

In the fall of 1972, an event that attracted national attention took place on the Illinois College campus—a speech by Secretary of Defense Melvin Laird, whose father had been a member of the Class of 1901. Before he rose to fame and

while he was quite young, he had come more than once to the campus with his father for alumni reunions.

Congressman Paul Findley had made arrangements with Secretary Laird for me to see him. The two of us went to Laird's office in the Pentagon where we were warmly received. He spoke of his father's experiences on the campus and readily agreed to find a time when he could visit the campus and receive an honorary degree after making a speech.

Because the nation was emerging from the student disorders partly associated with the Viet Nam War, those in charge of the military were not very popular with the radical left, and the security of governmental officials was carefully guarded. Laird and his party were to fly into Springfield and then travel by car to Jacksonville. Instead of using the more prestigious cars in which the secretary was expected to make the trip, he and a few special people in two old cars drove over by a back road.

That morning, a bomb squad from St. Louis came to the campus. They went over the chapel most thoroughly, even

Secretary of Defense Melvin Laird conducting a conference with student representatives in 1972. *Left to right:* Chairman of the Board William Clark '40, member of Congress Paul Findley '43, President Caine, Melvin Laird.

End of an Era

removing all the covers from light switches. They then sealed off the chapel. When the building was opened for the audience, numerous security people carefully looked over every person who entered.

Laird gave an excellent speech and was awarded an honorary degree. Afterwards, surrounded by guards, we walked across the campus to our home where he was to have lunch with some sixty to seventy people. The house was encircled by security men. I recall that two women walking ahead of us were stopped by an officer. They identified themselves as co-eds who were to help with the serving. The officer spoke to someone at our door on his walkie-talkie: "Two girls coming. They say they are waiting on tables. Check them out when they get to the door."

In his address, Laird had spoken of his hopes for a generation of peace backed by American might. After lunch, we had arranged to have him meet in the chapel with some forty student representatives of fourteen colleges and universities to answer their questions. There was a large audience, but only those special students had the privilege of the floor. A bank of television cameras filled one side of the front of the chapel. The three major networks and a number of individual stations covered the speech and the questioning. A friend in Montana wrote me that he had seen me on national television during the evening news broadcast.

In December 1971, death claimed chemistry professor Helmut C. Gutekunst, who would have retired at the end of the academic year. He had been at the College since 1957. William J. Sullivan '41, president of the State Life Insurance Company, Indianapolis, became a trustee in 1972.

At the annual meeting of the board in May 1972, I announced my retirement as of June 30, 1973, and a committee was appointed to find a new president. The budget adopted for the next year was $2.5 million. The first year of my presidency it had been about $450,000. Instead of the deficits of

the early fifties, the budget had been balanced every year and there was a surplus of more than $400,000 for the current year.

The year of retirement is a special time for anyone. It certainly was for me. Since the fall of 1927, the year of my graduation from college, when I became a science and speech teacher at Bryant, South Dakota, I had worked as an educator—forty-six years. For thirty-one years I had been a teacher and administrator in three colleges. Some reach retirement with a sigh of relief, and others treat it like a fatal disease. For me, it was a time of satisfaction. I thoroughly enjoyed what I was doing but in spite of those who say the opposite, age has its price and one does not have the energy to do the job at sixty-eight that one had at fifty, or even sixty. It was time for someone else to assume the burden that had been mine. I hoped my last year would be a good one, and it exceeded my sweetest dreams.

Even in my last year there was much to be done. Final plans for the new library were completed, and part of the cost of construction was raised. We had a particularly difficult time with the architects—more than with any other building. In the end, the library was a beautiful and very practical building. When I retired, $580,000 had been subscribed toward the cost of the new library with $470,000 of it in the bank drawing interest. At that time, the library cost estimate was $1 million, but when it was finished some years later, the cost had exceeded that estimate considerably.

One of the special events of the year was the visit of the Honorable Corneliu Bogdan, ambassador of the Socialist Republic of Rumania. The ambassador was accompanied by his secretary, who brought along his wife and small son. He gave three major speeches, to the students at a convocation, to the joint service clubs of Jacksonville, and to service clubs of Springfield. I remember that he implied that Rumania had little choice in many of its actions and policies because of Soviet domination. I recall, also, that the young son of the

secretary was often the center of attention at the reception for the party. He was a charming little boy. The secretary's wife was greatly pleased that a party of women, including Elizabeth, had her as a guest for lunch during the time of the joint service-club meeting. Ambassador Bogdan left the College a number of books about his country.

Crampton Hall celebrated its centennial in 1973. This venerable building had been about everything throughout its 100 years, but even when it was used partly for classes, it always housed students. It is the oldest structure in Illinois that has been used continuously for a dormitory.

Illinois College again secured a film series of considerable significance. The British Broadcasting Company had followed its enormously popular series "Civilisation" with another, also narrated by Kenneth Clark, called "Pioneers of Modern Painting." This six-part series dealt with the history of art and came to us under the sponsorship of the National Gallery of Art and the National Endowment for the Humanities.

Illinois College has a remarkable record of producing political leaders, ranging from William Jennings Bryan to precinct committeemen. Six alumni became state governors, two were U.S. senators, and twenty were U.S. representatives. We obtained photographs of all the senators and representatives and hung them in Tanner Library. Also, it was reported that year that 408 graduates of Illinois College were teaching in the public schools of Illinois.

At a meeting of the Morgan-Scott Medical Society on the campus and before a dinner at Baxter Hall, the society dedicated a plaque for the outside wall of Beecher Hall commemorating the fact that the first medical school in Illinois had been established there. It read, "In this building Illinois College established the first medical school in Illinois in 1841: opened to students in November, 1843; closed in 1848." At the dinner, Dr. Black gave a brief history of the medical school, and I delivered the main address on the contribution

of Illinois College to medicine in Illinois. I cited the fact that more than 300 doctors had taken premedical training here and that hundreds of dentists, nurses, and others in the healing arts had studied on this campus. Three successive physicians had served as secretary of the trustees since 1907.

Several men of the College achieved athletic distinction in the spring of 1973. William Sullivan established new records in both the 50- and 100-yard free-style swimming events and won both in the District 20 NAIA meets. Donald Steers pitched a no-hit game against Iowa Wesleyan. Two men won NAIA district events and competed in the nationals: Ronald Summers, who set records in both the discus and shot-put, and Bruce Penstone in the javelin. William Henry was medalist in the NAIA District golf meet, and William Kline was the District golf champion that fall.

There were four other retirements along with the Caines. Joseph Dixson reached retirement age, having served the College as Admissions Director since 1964. Two dormitory directors also retired. Mrs. Gwendolyn Lee had been in Ellis Hall since 1964. Mrs. Louise Becker began as director of Colonial Inn in 1960 and concluded her outstanding service in Crampton Hall. Mrs. Wilmith Gillham had been secretary to three presidents, having been first employed by President H. Gary Hudson in 1946. Her work had been of the highest order. I could not have found a better secretary. She was actually as much my assistant as my secretary.

The last semester of our years on the campus was an almost unbroken series of events honoring Elizabeth and me. Elizabeth's portrait was hung in Smith House, and an art prize was established in her name. As we made the last rounds of alumni meetings, we were the recipients of resolutions and awards. The Washington, D.C., Club presented a flag that had flown over the Capitol, provided by Representative Paul Findley. The Jacksonville Club gave us a beautiful limited-edition silver Audubon plate. The faculty held a dinner in our honor with tributes by Dr. and Mrs. Yeager and shorter

speeches by two of our sons, Dr. Stanley Caine, our youngest, and the oldest, Dr. Clifford Caine, who were invited back for the occasion. We were deeply moved by their kind words. Literary Societies honored us, and the I Association made me an honorary member and gave me a letter blanket—the kind awarded to graduating seniors.

The community also remembered us. The Chamber of Commerce sponsored a dinner for the family, after which a special convocation was held at MacMurray College with the faculties of the two institutions marching in the procession and the joint choirs providing music. The convocation speaker was Dr. James B. Holderman, executive director of the Illinois Board of Higher Education. Representatives of other groups brought greetings also. I was then awarded an honorary doctor of laws degree and became an alumnus of MacMurray College.

At Commencement, the trustees gave us a silver platter with the signature of each member engraved on it. Elizabeth was just able to attend the Commencement, having had her second operation for cancer not long before (her first was in 1970). These tokens of love and appreciation were particularly dear to us because many presidential administrations do not end in success, peace, and harmony. It had seldom happened at Illinois College. I was the tenth president since 1829, but in that more than 140-year period, I was only the third to retire peacefully. Two had died in office, and five had departed under strained circumstances. Being a college president is a hazardous occupation. Only Dr. Hudson and I had ever become presidents emeritus.

I "graduated" with the largest class ever to finish at Illinois: 181 students received bachelors of arts and science degrees. I was happy to have my long-time friend, distinguished alumnus Congressman Paul Findley, as the Commencement speaker. One of my last official acts was to confer on him the honorary degree of doctor of laws.

Inclement weather had driven us into the gymnasium and

At Commencement 1973, Chairman of the Board William Clark '40 presents the Caines with a sterling silver tray engraved with the signatures of members of the Board of Trustees.

the crowd was very large. I had a hard time getting through the last words I was to speak as the president of Illinois College. It was my nineteenth time to preside over a Commencement, for I had been an acting president at one before I came to Jacksonville. During the recessional, I saw tears in the eyes of many in the audience. There were tears in mine, too.

After Commencement, I had until the end of June to complete my work. At the request of President-elect Donald C. Mundinger, I hired the people who were to fill vacancies for the following fall and had some productive sessions with him in Chicago going over the situation of the College and telling him about the people with whom he would be working. I wrote scores of letters, left the new president notes on the continuing business, completed some records, and cleaned out desk drawers. Elizabeth and I had concluded that Jack-

End of an Era

sonville would be our home for the rest of our lives but that we should go away so as to give our successors an unhindered opportunity to become established. I had several opportunities to do consulting with church-related colleges on a yearly basis, so we stored our furniture for a year.

Our chapter in the leadership of Illinois College ended on the morning of Saturday, June 30, 1973. Elizabeth and I went for a last look at the grand house that had been not only our home but the scene of so many great events over the nearly eighteen years we had lived there. Without regrets, but with minds full of memories and with lumps in our throats, we locked the door and got into our loaded car. We drove around the campus for one last last time and headed out of town, not into the sunset but east into the sunlight on our way to visit one of our sons in Indiana before launching into a new venture.

8
Conclusion

I am sometimes asked what accomplishment of my administration gives me the most satisfaction. The answer is clear to me but will be more obvious at the end of a rather complicated explanation.

There are the physical improvements and additions on the campus that surpass by far those of any other administration: the three large dormitories, Ellis, Turner, and Pixley; Rammelkamp Chapel, Crispin Science Hall, and the Student Center; and the substantial addition to Baxter Dining Hall and the swimming pool addition to Memorial Gymnasium. These, along with the complete renovation of Sturtevant and Whipple and a completely new heating system for the entire campus, were the major construction projects. To that must be added the athletic fields, parking lots, tennis courts, replacement of hundreds of elms and other trees and shrubs, and two square blocks of new campus. While the physical improvements are not at the top of my list, the fact that they were all completed without leaving the College saddled with unpaid obligations is a source of pride.

Not many accomplishments were more important than the growth in enrollment—or more necessary. Starting below 300, the College increased its enrollment to a gross of 920. This increase was not achieved by relaxing admissions standards, which were actually raised, or by the addition of majors or courses catering to the less academic students. We admitted only those who had demonstrated their ability to

Conclusion

The Student Center is named by action of the trustees in honor of President Emeritus Caine. President Mundinger conducts the ceremony at Homecoming 1976. *Seated:* Elizabeth Caine and Galen Bremmer, president of the Student Forum.

do good college work. Quality was not sacrificed for quantity.

Certainly the change in the financial status was the most spectacular accomplishment. From a precarious and life-threatening situation, the College emerged as one of the most financially stable educational institutions in the state. Illinois College enjoyed an eighteen-year period of balanced operating budgets in contrast to the previous six years of deficit spending. Then, too, millions of dollars were raised and spent on buildings and campus improvements, and more millions set aside in the endowment. Renewed faith in the College and a program to promote bequests resulted in wills that would produce millions of dollars in new money in later

years. One example was the Pixley estate, which came to the College a few years after my retirement and added about $1.25 million to the endowment. This bequest was arranged years earlier. While the financial improvement was possibly the most spectacular achievement of my days as president, it was not my most satisfying accomplishment.

One aspect of my administration was a source of special satisfaction to me and to Elizabeth, who had such a large part in it: the conscious and successful attempt to enlarge college and community awareness of wider vistas. One facet of our efforts was an increase in international understanding. Quite a number of foreign-born scholars became members of the faculty. They added a dimension to education that could hardly have been achieved otherwise. The Visiting Asian Professors Program brought a considerable number of Far Eastern educators from various countries to the campus for extended periods of time. The Distinguished Visitors Program also included representatives of foreign nations. Examples of the latter were the ambassadors of Egypt, Rumania, West Germany, and Korea, along with others from foreign lands who lectured and visited with our people. Many Americans, of various occupations and interests, also visited our campus through the program. During all those years, a stream of persons of various nationalities, backgrounds, vocations, and opinions brought their views and convictions for consideration by students, faculty, and the community.

In the area of national government alone the list of visitors is impressive. These people included three members of presidential cabinets, State Department teams, two Illinois governors, and several members of Congress. While I myself did not teach any classes, I took pride in the fact that I used my influence directly to bring a wealth of talent to the campus, thus enhancing liberal learning.

The heart of the educational program is the faculty, and the quality of a college can hardly rise above the quality of its faculty. One of the most attractive aspects of Illinois Col-

Conclusion

lege, as I considered the offer to be its president, was the strength of the faculty. During this period of great growth, nothing was harder to maintain than a good faculty. I am proud that the situations of the faculty improved greatly by my efforts. Salaries naturally went up, but the relative pay of professors was also much higher at the end than at the beginning of my tenure. Faculty members received better fringe benefits including more insurance, greater retirement benefits, money for travel and sabbaticals, and far better equipment and facilities.

Above even this as a source of satisfaction, as I review the record, is the maintenance and enhancement of the good name of the College during a period in which their special constituencies turned against many institutions. Honor and decency were not compromised by disorder and destruction on our campus. If there is any place in the world where reason should prevail, it is at an academic institution. It did so at Illinois College, and the institution emerged from a tragic era with its good name intact. Maintaining the College's reputation was of enormous importance in every way but especially in the securing of gifts and bequests from people of means who, for the most part, are conservative in their views.

Finally, I can best illustrate the major achievement of my administration by retelling a memorable incident. General Harold K. Johnson was Chief of Staff of the U.S. Army in 1965. He had been a low-ranking officer serving in the Philippines when the Japanese attacked. He had survived the Corregidor siege and the Death March after the Bataan surrender and endured three and one-half years as a prisoner of war. Willis Hawkins '36, who had served as Assistant Secretary of the Army, told me that General Johnson was the only recent Chief of Staff who never had a major command before becoming Chief of Staff. His selection for that important post resulted from his actions as a prisoner of war in Japan. Johnson was the highest ranking officer in the prison camp to which he was assigned. The Japanese had never had expe-

The Illinois College Faculty of 1972-1973. *Front row, left to right:* Grace H. Cleary, G. Jack Mann, Lynette H. Seator, Charles E. Frank, Carole M. Ryan, Wallace N. Jamison, L. Vernon Caine, J. T. Van Horn, Don P. Filson, Ts'ing-Hi Tong, Raymond A. Ford, Harold S. Leam. *Row 2:* J. Robert Smith, Frederick Pilcher, Loren D. Moehn, Ann M. Larson, Marion S. McGeath, Isabelle Boehme, Elizabeth R. Zeigler, William M. Cross, Glenn F. Blackwood, Doris B. Hopper, Donald R. Tracey, Anthony M. Zaleski, Louis F. Meek. *Row 3:* Philip E. Bradish, Lawrence G. Bienert, Edgar A. Franz, James E. Davis, Richard L. Pratt, Karen E. Cozart, Louise Rainbolt, Geraldine Staley, Richard T. Fry, David H. Koss, Carey H. Kirk, Donald R. Eldred, Richard F. Rogal. *Row 4:* James O. Desreumaux, John N. Langfitt, George W. Horton, Jr., Erwin C. Bleckley, Ruth Fosnaugh, Wilbur S. Chien, Iver F. Yeager, Malcolm F. Stewart, Ruth E. F. Bump, John P. Sorenson, Joseph D. Dixson, Bennett C. Moulder, Robert J. Evans, Laurence C. Judd. *Not pictured:* William Anderson, E. Joseph Brooks, Dorothy Buchanan, Richard Graber, William Merris, Ethel Seybold, Vidyapati Singh, and part-time faculty members.

rience with large numbers of prisoners, and their camps were terrible places, full of disorder and suffering.

Because the camp in which he was held was so much better run and caused so much less trouble, the Japanese used Johnson as the prisoner negotiator in bringing some order out of their other prisoner-of-war installations. His ability and wisdom and his skill in representing the prisoners saved the lives of many Americans and earned him commendation. This ex-

Conclusion

hibition of statesmanship and leadership ability was eventually to result in his appointment as Chief of Staff.

Representative Paul Findley had suggested Johnson as a Commencement speaker and arranged for me to see Johnson so that I might issue the invitation. Instead of a brief appointment, General Johnson invited our two alumni congressmen, Findley and Charlotte Reid, and me to have lunch with him at the Pentagon in his office. We were only partly through the delightful meal when the two representatives were called back to cast their votes on a critical issue in the House. The two of us continued our conversation as we ate.

I asked General Johnson what his most difficult task was as Chief of Staff. He said the problem was that various segments of the service always vied for special consideration. His most difficult job was to see that all elements went forward together.

My answer to the inquiry of what gives me the deepest satisfaction as the leader of Illinois College during my years of responsibility for its welfare is that the gains were achieved in all parts of the institution. The improvement was not only in academics, or in international understanding, or in monetary gains, or in construction. It was in unity, spiritual resources, better-compensated professors, well-maintained buildings and grounds, more equipment, better students, and better athletic facilities. Advances occurred on all fronts. High on the long list was the respect of its neighbors and the love of its constituency. Illinois College would go on to new heights in the years ahead.

More than a decade has passed into history since the last of the events recorded here took place. Under the leadership of President Mundinger, my successor, the College has moved ahead at an undiminished pace. Its contribution to the strength of our nation and the attempt of mankind to move to a higher level has not declined.

There is much in the world to discourage even those who

are most optimistic. Christian and liberating institutions such as Illinois College keep hope alive. Their priceless contribution to America's greatness and its ennobling influence have paid rich dividends for those who invested their lives and their resources in making this nation what it is.

Much has happened since the day I retired. Most formidable to me was the passing of Elizabeth after ten years of valiant struggle against cancer. She had much to do with the successes of our years here. She was loved by everybody because she was their friend. She was a priceless asset to the College. She was also a good wife and mother, and our greatest mutual joy was in the singularly useful lives of our three sons. I think of her every day and am thankful.

Appendixes
Index

Appendix A
To Heights Beyond:
The Inaugural Address, October 19, 1956

There is much here that does not meet the eye. If we think we are performing only a current academic chore, we fail completely to understand the significance of this occasion. I am the tenth to assume the office of president of Illinois College in the 128 years since its opening in 1829, but all that has happened to this college in that long span has relevancy to this event. No appraisal of either the present or the future will be valid without a look at the past, and no one is worthy of the leadership which I have assumed who at a moment like this does not feel a heavy responsibility to the men and women who wrought the substance of a dream and who in this and previous generations have had a part in the development of this old and honorable college.

Back in the days when Andrew Jackson was president, when those who fought in the War of 1812 were no older than the present veterans of World War II, a remarkable young Presbyterian minister, John M. Ellis, was seeking to establish in this area a "seminary of learning." This he regarded as one of the most needed instruments for the advancement of the cause of Christ on this frontier. His efforts came to the attention of some young men at Yale University who had dedicated their lives to carrying the Gospel to far-off places. This "Yale Band" along with John M. Ellis were the founders of the College. History records that when these young men made their decision to come here, "Illinois was less known and less accessible than the foreign fields of Asia." Fired with the desire to promote "religion and learning," these young men of two great denominations established the first college in Illinois to grant a degree and one of the earliest institutions of higher learning west of the Alleghenies.

Appendix A

The first of my predecessors was the Reverend Edward Beecher, who left the secure and comfortable pastorate of the great Park Street Church of Boston to undertake an adventure of faith on the limitless prairie of the vast and almost empty Midwest. Beginning with his brother, Henry Ward Beecher, and his sister, Harriet Beecher Stowe, he brought to this campus such other national figures as Ralph Waldo Emerson and Amos Bronson Alcott. This procession of great Americans included Daniel Webster, Stephen A. Douglas, and the immortal Abraham Lincoln.

Time will not permit mention, much less recounting, the contributions of my nine distinguished predecessors, but I must at least mention the long and brilliant administration of Dr. Charles Henry Rammelkamp, who presided over the destinies of this college from 1905 to 1932. During his time, the endowment went over the million-dollar mark, two buildings were erected, and a Phi Beta Kappa chapter was installed. We are honored to have with us still the widow of this great man, who, as his helpmate and in her own right, deserves our thanks and appreciation.

It seems only fair to say that while a president is necessary and without him a college flounders, the work of the teacher is of primary importance. I have said on several occasions to the faculty that those of us who are in administrative positions are simply "auxiliary enterprises." The essential job here, and at any college, is teaching. This college has a proud tradition of great teachers. They are with us today and they have been throughout all the generations. It strikes me as especially appropriate that most of the buildings on this campus are named not after philanthropists but educators.

At a time like this, one must also add a word of appreciation for that large group of men and women who have served Illinois College in the capacity of trustees and financial supporters. There is little glory and much worry in the work of a trustee. Their role at Illinois College has never been an easy one. To those of this generation we owe a special debt of gratitude for having charted the course of this college during difficult days. They, along with this larger group, which includes many here present, who from generous hearts erected these buildings, provided the facilities, and balanced the budgets over a century and a quarter, are the unsung heroes of Illinois College.

To Heights Beyond

Intriguing as the past is, Shakespeare reminds us that "What's past is prologue." If we are to be worthy of those who gave us this goodly heritage, we shall not prove so unless we work in the present and dream for the future.

Those who have come to know me in the brief time I have lived in Jacksonville must be aware that I will not make the too common mistakes of new administrators in thinking that progress begins where I came in. I am not here to outline any grandiose plans to bring to pass greater advance in the next few years than came about in the combined lifetimes of my predecessors. We are going ahead. We have enormous resources of good will among those who know us. We have a good endowment, a beautiful campus, a loyal and unusually distinguished body of alumni, an academic reputation well above the average as attested to by a Phi Beta Kappa chapter. We also have our needs: a women's dormitory to be built immediately, a science building, a new chapel, toward which we already have $80,000. We need the continued, regular and generous contributions of friends to give us annually the extra funds we must have to balance the budget, as we did last year.

I shall say no more about these obvious needs as I hasten to speak of those things less tangible, but more vital, which affect the heart and soul of the college, and, in the long run, determine whether or not we are worthy of our heritage and true to the sacrifices of those who make this event possible. I do not say those are the paramount issues in American education, nor do I imply that this should be the platform on which all college administrators should stand, but I do feel that these are among the most fundamental obligations which rest upon the leadership of Illinois College at this critical juncture in its life and in the life of America and a free world.

(1) The obligation to enlist and inspire young men and women in the never-ending struggle for freedom, justice, and peace, a struggle which has engaged the attention of every generation of Americans.

Nobody here ever heard of Pike Clinton Ross or John L. McConnell, but both were Illinois College men and one served as a private and one as a captain in the Mexican War. Ever since, when peaceful methods seem to have failed and when "the right was more precious than peace," men from this college have answered the call

Appendix A

of their country. Six or eight of them have attained the "general" rank. Many have given the "last full measure of devotion," but it is not that men of this and future generations will be ready for some Gettysburg, San Juan Hill, Flanders Field, or Coral Sea that I speak.

Some of our visitors may have come across the plaque near the tennis court which marks the place where students of Illinois College met in protest over the mob action against the abolitionist Lovejoy at Alton. So involved were students and faculty on the side of freedom in the critical days before the Civil War that William Herndon, later Abraham Lincoln's law partner, was taken out of Illinois College by his father in order to remove him from what seemed to be intemperate antislavery influence. So positive was the feeling at Illinois College on the great moral issue of slavery that Judge T. J. C. Fagg of Missouri, Illinois College Class of 1842, wrote as the war clouds gathered in that slave-holding territory in which he lived, "The greatest opposition I had to contend with in my professional, political, and social life here in Missouri was the fact that I had graduated from Illinois College."

It was a young man, only fifteen years out of Illinois College after spending six years on this campus and graduating from Whipple Academy in 1877 and from the College with the class of 1881, who rocketed to fame with an oration that is remembered even today. At the national political convention of one of the major parties in 1896, he concluded his memorable speech with these words, "You shall not press down upon the brow of labor this crown of thorns. You shall not crucify mankind upon a cross of gold." William Jennings Bryan, who was to be the standard bearer in three campaigns for the presidency and later to become secretary of state, was a man who served peace and justice according to the dictates of his conscience. Now I suspect that if I had been alive and a voter I would not have been on his side. I recite these facts about the antislave feeling and the social and economic interests of other days to exemplify the precious tradition of Illinois College which deserves to live forever, a genuine concern for problems of human welfare. Slavery has long since vanished and the "cross of gold" has found refuge at Fort Knox, but when such issues as desegregation still harass America and when there are in other lands "teeming masses yearning to breathe free," the battle call for freedom, justice, and

peace still must be sounded in all the free institutions of America, including this college, to awaken the minds and souls of young men and women as to their role as participants in the struggle of mankind to emerge from the swamps of fear and prejudice and to take man's rightful place, which is only a little lower than the angels.

(2) We must acknowledge and willingly accept the fact of the necessity of change. This has ever been true. What was good yesterday is not good enough today.

> *New occasions teach new duties,*
> *Time makes ancient good uncouth;*
> *We must upward be and onward,*
> *Who would keep abreast of truth.*

It is said that when Adam and Eve were being driven from the Garden of Eden, the first man said to his mate, "My dear, we are living in an age of transition." So it has ever been. Wisdom consists of foreseeing and planning for new developments and not being forced by circumstances to make changes simply to survive. "Where there is no vision, people perish." So do institutions.

I advocate the forward look, the cautious venture, the willingness to be among the first in the procession. This is good traditional Illinois College doctrine. This college came into being because of venturesome souls. Illinois College established the first medical school in the state, but the venture did not not succeed and so it was abandoned with no discredit to the College. For seventy-four years this was a men's college and many predicted fatal consequences if women were admitted to "Old Illinois." Now fifty-four years later even our academic mother, Yale University, is considering coeducation, our way, as the sounder system. Once Illinois College had a strong department of agriculture which outlived its usefulness and was dropped. There are those who deplored the passing of Greek and Latin from the center of liberal arts education, but the same inexorable decline of the classical influence goes on in architecture, art, and philosophy. Science was on the fringes of academic respectability in the early days of this institution. Richard Yates, our first graduate and governor of the state of Illinois during the Civil War, took the course prescribed for all students, including astronomy and plenty of mathematics, but he did not

have a single hour of what is the present program in the physical or biological sciences; none was offered.

I would remind you also that it is not now and never has been good American educational doctrine to believe that practical education is not worthy of a place in a liberal arts curriculum. Yale, Harvard, and Princeton were established for vocational reasons—that the people might have educated ministers. It is quite true that today some institutions have gone to absurd length to set up courses in insignificant and nonacademic subject matter. The story is told of the boy in such a college who, wishing to improve a low grade average, signed up for basket weaving and was distressed to discover that the enrolling of three Navajo Indians dislocated the anticipated grading curve and left him still at a point of mediocrity. It has been said, not without at least some reason, that certain courses in teacher training institutions have been a grain of truth in a bushel of rubbish, but it does not follow that it is more noble to teach history to prospective lawyers than to prospective high-school teachers, or that engineering drawing is more legitimately in the liberal arts college than is medical technology, or the history of art more respectable than the history of education.

I favor as best for us and our people a rather strict liberal arts program, but we do not degrade liberal arts when we serve the needs of the kind of students we want most. I need not tell any parent or educator that the most alert, the most thoughtful, and the most able student wants to see in his education some tangible progress toward his vocational goal.

(3) We must continue to emphasize the paramount importance of scholarship; to recognize that Illinois College is essentially an intellectual community. It seems strange that such a thing need be said at any college or at any time, but the issue of who ought to go to college is a very live one today. There are a good many institutions who will admit anyone with a high-school diploma. Illinois College is a far cry from that. It is sometimes argued that every student benefits from exposure to college even though his intellectual interests and capabilities are such that he will not succeed as a serious student. Even if that is true, it is not a valid reason for unrestricted college admission. It is most unfortunate that a student with an able mind and a desire for higher education is denied that oppor-

tunity because of circumstances beyond his control. But there is no obligation on the part of society to provide institutions of higher learning for those who have neither the wit nor the incentive for making proper use of such an opportunity.

There is another aspect to the idea that the college is the intellectual community. Some colleges while professing to be interested primarily in scholarship nevertheless on Friday nights or Saturday afternoons in the fall demonstrate conclusively that to them the frosting is more important than the cake. It seems absurd that colleges or universities of any size should spend vast amounts of time and money competing for the services of brawny, agile physical specimens with little or no regard for their intellectual ability or interest in academic pursuits.

At Illinois College we shall continue the time-honored policy of admitting persons without regard for race or color, and we shall judge their admission scrupulously on the basis of intellectual ability and character. We shall promote worthy extracurricular activities including intercollegiate athletics which I favor, but we shall not permit the tail to wag the dog.

(4) Illinois College has the obligation to be Christian. This resolution deserves our special attention, but let it not be misunderstood.

I am a strong advocate of public schools and have the highest regard for tax-supported education at all levels. This nation could never have come to its present stature without our great public institutions. We are proud that Jonathan B. Turner, a professor at Illinois College, became the father of the University of Illinois and the originator of the land-grant college idea which resulted in the establishment of so many of our great public universities. America needs both types of institutions. It would be no less a catastrophe to lose the independent colleges than the tax-supported institutions. We need not decide which is the more important; both are necessary.

There are ample reasons for the maintenance of independent colleges without religious profession, but the non-tax-supported college loses one of its most valid reasons for being when it eliminates its Christian emphasis. As far as I am concerned, I doubt whether the sacrifice, the worry, and the sweat necessary to maintain this

Appendix A

college are justified if we do not hold central the Christian concern of our founding fathers. Let the taxpayers take care of higher education if we do no more than duplicate the public program.

Illinois College came into being because a Christian missionary and some young Christians at Yale heard a call from God to establish an institution "of religion and learning." The seal of the College which appears on today's program was suggested by the first president and adopted by the trustees. In these words, the trustees explained the meaning of the seal: "The word of God is the sure foundation of science, true liberty and religion, the three pillars of the social system, and these alone can maintain inviolate our laws and rights." This statement is, I believe, profoundly true. To advocate a Christian environment and a Christian emphasis is not only to hold with the higher traditions of this and other church-related colleges, but it is also to be the most truly patriotic and the most humanitarian. Our presidents from Washington down through Lincoln to Dwight D. Eisenhower have gratefully and publicly acknowledged in official statements that the guidance of God was the primary factor in America's coming into being and its rise to power and prestige. We make the greatest contribution to the welfare of humanity not simply by transmitting or advancing knowledge, but we fulfill our destiny best when we develop along with knowledge the minds and hearts of young men and women to hear above the call of profit, fame, or pleasure, the voices of God speaking to them. "The fear of the Lord is the beginning of wisdom." A key question for men and nations continues to be "What does it profit a man if he gain the whole world and lose his own soul?" We are committed by heritage and by reason to raise these issues along with many that are less eternal.

We have the privilege of being linked by birth and breeding with bonds stronger than contracts, with two great denominations, the Congregational Christian Churches and the Presbyterian Church in the U.S.A. We gladly maintain standards which they approve, and we are grateful for the fact that something is expected of us because of our associations with these denominations. We are still as free as we wish to be. Students of all denominations are welcome here. It is not the business of the denominations to minister only to their own. This College represents a share of the great work of higher education as carried on for all people. It is not of, by, or for

To Heights Beyond

the Congregationalists or the Presbyterians, but we are a Christian college and that we shall continue so to be.

In accepting the leadership of this college, my prayer is that of the little Negro boy who grew up around the kitchen of an old plantation. He liked molasses and used to reach into the barrel that he might lick the sweetness from his chubby fingers. One day finding the molasses low, he balanced himself on the rim of the barrel and leaning too far down plunged headfirst into the depth. As he fell he prayed, "Lord give me capacity equal to my opportunity." So pray I.

Illinois College stands at the threshold of a new day rich in opportunity for growth in service to God and man. By all odds this should be the finest chapter in the long history. Let us, as we look back on what has been and move forward into an unknown future, resolve that with God's help this College shall continue to be a significant constructive force. May we so labor here that in some future day when we are but history, our record will be such as to inspire those who come after us to achievements of service far greater than even our present dreams. May future generations think of us also when they close the alma mater with these words:

May the lamps thy fathers lighted
Lead thee e'er to heights beyond.

Appendix B
Who Runs the College?

Without a doubt the most common current concern expressed by alumni and friends of this and other colleges has to do with the conduct and attitude of students in recent times. Although campus disorders have been exaggerated and greatly overpublicized by the news media, it is undeniable that recent events on many campuses have been a disgrace to the nation. The excesses of a few students on a few campuses have aroused the indignation of the overwhelming majority of thinking Americans.

The disorderly conduct of certain student groups and the general unrest in this college generation is not without some underlying causes. These young people have been reared permissively in a society of abundance so that it is extremely difficult for them to mature normally. Many are overprivileged, ungrateful for what is done for them, and nearly all are concerned about the draft, the justification for the war in Vietnam, and tensions in society not of their own making. Unfortunately this college generation has also been taught, often by some of the most high-minded people in America, that demonstrations, sit-ins, and other nonviolent disturbances of the peace are tolerable and sometimes even noble. It remains true, however, that no amount of understanding of good or bad reasons for the action of certain students excuses what has taken place.

At Illinois College and others of its type, certain things should be abundantly clear. First, enrollment in a non–tax supported college is a privilege and not a right. A college may be whatever it chooses to be, and when a student enrolls, he has in effect entered into an implied contract to operate within the framework of the institution. A college may deny to its students the right to operate

Who Runs the College?

an automobile, require him to be vaccinated or to learn to swim, to refrain from smoking on the campus, or to go to chapel—all these things are required at some institutions. If a student is fundamentally opposed to regulations clearly announced, his option is to register somewhere else.

The legal responsibility for the operation of a college is inescapably in the hands of the trustees. As in the case of the Charter and By-Laws of this institution, the president and the faculty have some prescribed roles. Those who are legally appointed to carry out such functions cannot do otherwise. It is the practice here to use students in advisory capacity on almost all committees and to maintain an open door policy so that students may have access to any faculty member or officer of the College, including the president, but when final decisions must be made, they are made solely by those whose legal or delegated powers have been specifically set forth.

In considering changes of any nature at a college, it must be remembered that the student body of any given year makes up only a fraction of what might be "the college." There are the thousands of alumni of other years. There are the friends and benefactors who have provided the buildings and the endowment. Of most importance is the fact that there are those yet unborn who will some day attend the institution. Any administrator worthy of his salt is concerned as much about the college ten years from now as of today. It is unthinkable that the whims of a particular student body in any given year should adversely reflect on 139 years of experience of this institution or should put in jeopardy the progress or contribution that the College will be making in the 1970s and 1980s.

Another idea that needs serious promotion at any institution of higher learning is that an academic institution ought to be ruled by reason and not by force either violent or nonviolent. The changes which are always taking place should come about as the result of conferences and not by confrontation. If education is good for anything, it ought to make people reasonable in what they do. Since nearly all students at a college of this type are reasonable human beings, there is no excuse for a few malcontents to be permitted to disturb the peace which is so essential to learning. Differences of opinion are the stock in trade of an educational institution, but

tolerance and reasonableness are also essential. Illinois College has been fortunate in having a student body made up of those who are overwhelmingly motivated by good will and reason. This is the way it ought to be.

Appendix C
Commencement Remarks to the Class of 1973

I am happy to be able to report for the eighteenth consecutive year that we have better than a balanced budget. Good progress is being made toward securing the funds necessary for the new library which will be constructed as soon as the money is available. I am pleased to say, also, that we have experienced a very good year, sufficiently tranquil to carry on good learning but lively enough to be interesting.

It is with satisfaction and thankfulness that I turn over to my successor a college not floundering or of an uncertain future, but ready for the new challenges of changing times. We who care much for Illinois College look back with considerable satisfaction upon the record of recent years. The trustees have done well in their choices during the recent turbulent times unprecedented in college history. This wisdom is manifested in the financial stability which is unequaled in the long history of the college and is especially noteworthy when a great many good colleges are teetering on the brink of financial disaster.

Greatly to be coveted also is the high regard in which this college is held even by its near neighbors who know it for what it is and the ever growing respect it continues to generate as the result of the accomplishments of its alumni. I hope that in the years ahead, while much will change in practice and procedures, the basic mission of the college will not be altered. It is a door of opportunity for any who are able and willing to submit to its disciplines. May it continue to be concerned not only with the dispersion of knowledge but also with advancement of character and spiritual insights. May it always be a Christian liberal arts college with a concerned faculty and staff and a family feeling that extends to alumni and neighbors

Appendix C

as is so well demonstrated at these exercises today and at the Osage Orange Picnic and those other lovely ties which bring together men and women of good will on this beautiful campus.

My last word is to you, the Class of 1973, with which Elizabeth and I graduate. Two dates will linger in my memory as long as I live. One is 1927, the year I was graduated from college, and the other is 1973 when another kind of college career ends for me. When I look at you, the largest class ever to be graduated from Illinois College, I see also all those others who over eighteen years have sat where you sit and recall a fragment of a poem in which an alumnus speaks as he returns to his alma mater:

I used
To pause here, so, alone free as a bird,
And see the unseen, hear sounds never heard.
Now in this time of life, I lift this hand
To call back from the shadows all my band
Who lived upon this hill, drank at these springs,
And traded college days for songs and wings.

Ten presidents have served Illinois College in its 144 years, and Commencements date back to 1835. I was somewhat shocked to discover that I have awarded degrees to more than 40 percent of all who have been graduated here.

The situation into which your predecessors have gone from Commencement has fluctuated greatly. There was a time when most of the young men went into military service. There was a time when anyone who was qualified, and sometimes even not qualified, could have a teaching job without asking. But no more. You face a situation much more like that of most of the alumni in this audience at your age.

We do not see you off into a world of tranquility or ease. I do not predict or even hope for you a world without strife or heartache. There are wrongs to be righted and battles to be fought. You have miles to go before you sleep. My hope is that on this campus you have caught the vision of the kind of world that ought to be and have resolved to do your part to make the dream a reality. May you learn how to live in a world of dissonance without adding to the confusion. May you be an instrument of peace. As one who has

Commencement Remarks

been an active participant in the agonies of humanity over a lifetime in a time of world history characterized by enormous changes and boiling troubles, I pass on to you the role of reconciliation and healing which is the responsibility of all Christians and other civilized men. I ask you to seek God's guidance in making your years count for something in a world that desperately needs such talents.

In closing, I want to repeat a story I used in my inauguration address back in 1956. It applied to me then, and I hope now it will apply to you. You are in a position similar to that of a small Negro boy who lived around the kitchen where his mother worked on a plantation before what Southerners called "the War between the States." The little fellow dearly loved molasses, which he would lick from the chubby fingers he dipped in the barrel. Once when the barrel was more than half empty he climbed upon a chair, leaned too far, and plunged headfirst into the sticky depths. As he fell he prayed, "Lord, give me capacity equal to my opportunity." This, too, should be your prayer.

So I commend you to the unknown future full of wonder and surprise, heartaches, disappointments, triumphs, joys, and labor; to all the uncertainties of other generations and some more, to dreams and to God. The future is for you. You will live in the twenty-first century when my generation will be but a memory and a foundation and yours will be whatever power and glory there is. For it is as the ancient writer said,

One generation passeth away and another generation cometh, but the earth abideth forever. The sun also riseth and the sun goeth down and hasteneth to a place where he arose. All rivers run into the sea, yet the sea is not full. Unto the place from whence they come, thither they return again and there is nothing new under the sun.

But it will be new for you, and as you go out and as we separate from the campus life of this college, though never from its influence, may the Lord bless each of us and Illinois College.

INDEX

Adams, Samuel, 136
Affiliated Artists Program, 137
Akers, Milburn, 116
Albion College, 80
Alumni Association, 13, 15, 33, 72
Alumni Fund, 13, 84
Alumni Quarterly, 14, 51
American Council On Education, 147
Art Association, 108
Associated Colleges of Illinois, 7, 84
Association of American Colleges, 25, 114, 135, 140
Auh, Chun-Suk, 85, 86, 118

Babson, Roger, 42, 43, 44
Bach, Marcus, 28
Badger, John, 25
Barlow, Charles, 156
Barnes, Clifford Webster, 26, 107
Barnes, James, 45
Baus, Joseph, 30
Baxter, George, 15, 46, 67, 68, 123
Baxter Hall, 3, 27, 31, 49, 50, 105, 117, 143, 168
Beadle, George W., 109
Becker, Louise, 42, 69, 164
Beecher, Edward, 109, 149
Beecher, John, 85
Beecher Hall, 8, 33, 134
Bellatti, Mrs. Walter, 46
Bellatti, Ruth, 107
Bellatti, Walter, 46, 75
Bellatti, Walter R., 88

Bell Laboratories, 28
Benton, Thomas Hart, 120, 121
Bienert, Lawrence G., 117
Black, C. Ellsworth, 1, 2, 3, 4, 15, 92, 156, 163
Blackburn College, 38
Board of Christian Education, Presbyterian, 30
Bogdan, Corneliu, 162, 163
Bohan, Ruth, 146
Bradish, Philip, 117
Brewster, Kingman, 78
Brooks, Joe, 101, 102
Bruggeman, Walter, 152
Bryan, Charles, 53
Bryan, William Jennings, 36, 53, 73, 130, 163
Bump, Ruth, 36, 94
Burns, Arthur, 142
Byrom, Mrs. Frank F., 69, 108

CACHE, 66, 84
Caine, Alan, 1, 47, 119
Caine, Clifford, 1, 47, 165
Caine, Elizabeth, 7, 25, 26, 34, 46, 96, 111, 158, 164, 166, 167, 174
Caine, Stanley, 1, 7, 47, 165
Campbell, Julia, 122
Capps, Edward, 13
Capps, Joseph, 109
Capps, Julian, 80
Capps, Robert, 3, 109, 123, 137
Capps, Stephen, 80
Carleton College, 46
Carnegie Foundation, 25
Carriel, C. A., 79

193

Index

Catton, Bruce, 45, 46
Cellini, William, 143
Central Methodist College, 102
Chamber of Commerce, 165
Chicago, University of, 11, 25, 49, 53, 65, 75, 86, 109, 112
Chicago Theological Seminary, 11, 80, 122
Chien, Wilbur, 59, 118
Chung, Paul, 140
Civil War, 54
Civil War Roundtable, 45
Clark, Henry, 123
Clark, John, 131
Clark, Kenneth, 155, 163
Clark, William, 123
Clifford, Edward, 46
Colonial Inn, 32, 58, 106, 130, 164
Columbia University, 21, 115
Comments, 139
Congregational and Congregational Christian Churches, 29, 30, 37, 42, 49, 71, 114, 115, 122
Conservatory of Music, 107
Craig, Gordon, 95
Crain, Douglas, 75
Crampton Hall, 11, 32, 34, 42, 51, 58, 106, 163, 164, 168
Crawford, Kenneth, 152
Crispin, Egerton, 67, 68
Crispin Science Hall, 34, 35, 68, 73, 88, 106, 137, 159
Culver Stockton College, 104, 120, 123

Damsgaard, Conrad, 14
Damsgaard, Patricia, 14, 24
Danskin, Kenneth, 145
da Vinci, Leonardo, 98
Day, James, 116
Day, J. Edward, 87
Department of Housing and Urban Development. *See* Housing and Home Finance Agency (HHFA)

DePauw University, 158, 159
DeRyke, Willis, 88
Dickerson, Ray, 143
Dillon, Doris, 13, 14
Dirksen, Everett, 147
Distinguished Visitors Program, 28, 85, 110, 170
Distler, Theodore A., 140
Dixson, Joseph, 164
Douglas, Paul, 53, 75
Dreer, Herman, 93
DuBois, Mignon, 23
Dubuque University, 123
Dummer, E. Heyse, 75
Dunbaugh, Harry, 30, 46, 71, 73, 122, 123, 145
Duncan, Clyde, 79

Eldred, Donald, 71
Eliot, Ray (Nuspickel), 69
Elliott, F. Osborne, 60
Elliott, Frank, 3
Ellis, John, 33
Ellis Hall, 33, 34, 44, 51, 58, 106, 164, 168
Elmhurst College, 38, 123
Engle, Paul, 28
Eppenberger, Emily, 93

Fauth, Robert, 152
Fayerweather House, 11, 32, 34, 58, 106, 130, 155
Federal Bureau of Investigation, 83
Federal Hall, 33, 35, 105, 106
Federation of Illinois Colleges and Universities, 109
Ferguson, Charles, 28, 86
Filson, Don, 59, 88
Filson, Floyd, 88
Findley, Paul, 85, 88, 94, 95, 98, 116, 147, 151, 160, 164, 165, 173
Findley, William, 152
Ford Foundation, 12, 57, 63
Forward Step, 82, 149
Frackelton, Mrs. Robert, 135

Index

Frank, Charles, 35
Franz, Edgar, 120
French, Marian, 102
Friend, Shirley, 149
Fry, Richard, 130
Fulbright Fellowship, 53, 83, 85, 88, 123
Funk, Donald, 39

Gardner, William, 26, 71
Gardner Hall, 32, 34, 40, 51, 58, 106
Garratt, Willard, 46, 152
Garrison, George H., 116
Ghorbal, Ashraf, 155, 156
GI Bill, 14, 20, 23, 35, 53, 55, 106, 154
Gibson, Hugh, 10
Gillham, Wilmuth, 9, 12, 164
Grange, Red, 4
Gutekunst, Helmut C., 161

Hackett, Helen, 119
Hardin, Clifford, 25
Hart, Arthur, 53, 60
Hartman, Beatrice, 33
Hartman, Ray, 3
Hartman, Robert, 60, 66, 88
Harvard University, 20, 25, 29, 141
Hastings, W. T., 31
Hawkins, Willis, 171
Henry, David, 78
Henry, William, 164
Hess, Lyndle, 73, 150
Hickey, Robert, 104
High, Stanley, 28
Hildner, Ernest, Jr., 6, 18, 49, 70, 86, 154, 157
Holderman, James B., 165
Horton, George, 3, 46, 83, 94
Horton, William, 137
Hoskins, Fred, 3, 7, 11, 20, 21, 30, 71, 80, 122, 130
Housing and Home Finance Agency (HHFA), 9, 32, 34, 35, 105

Hudson, Gary, 30, 130, 164, 165
Humphrey, Hubert H., 114
Hurrelbrink, Gale, 82

IBM, 98
Illinois, University of, 29, 61, 69, 78, 79
Illinois Power Co., 95
Illinois State Normal (University), 77, 79
Independent College Fund of America, 65, 84
Iowa Wesleyan, 123

Jacksonville Female Academy, 25, 33, 53, 107
Jacksonville Journal Courier, 78
Jamestown College, 1, 64, 66
Jamison, Wallace N., 153
Johnson, Harold K., 116, 171, 173
Johnson, Lyndon B., 35, 113
Johnson, Edward, 152
John XXIII, Pope, 119
Jones, Hiram, 26
Jones, Ray Carlton, 137
Jones Hall, 8, 17, 33, 34, 40, 53, 106
Judd, Walter, 28, 121
Junior Academy of Science, 134

Kennedy, John F., 35, 86, 87, 92, 119
Kerner, Otto, 76, 96, 98
Ketchledge, Raymond, 28
Kim, Dong Jo, 140, 141, 142, 143
Kinchloe, Susan, 122
Kiwanis Club, 69
Kline, William, 164
Knox College, 25, 38
Kohr, Russell, 1, 2
Kuhfuss, William M., 79
Kund, Harold, 82
Kuster, Ulrich, 82

Laird, Melvin, 27, 159, 160, 161
Lake Forest College, 1, 38

Index

Leam, Harold, 130
Lebkeucher, Linda, 82
Lee, Gwendolyn, 164
Lincoln, Abraham, 29, 45, 54, 78, 98
Lincoln Academy, 96
Lincoln Land Community College, 62
Lindenwood College, 123
Linnenburger, Alta, 122
Lohman, Carol, 33
Lovejoy, Elijah P., 149

Macalester College, 1, 4, 21, 28, 66
McCormick Theological Seminary, 59, 88
McGovern, George, 75, 121
McGrath, Earl, 115
McKendree College, 134
MacMurray College, 5, 6, 23, 47, 85, 103, 104, 106, 107, 118, 131, 132, 133, 134, 140, 165
McNamara, Carole Ann (Carole McNamara Ryan), 53, 83, 94)
McWard, Gail E., 156
Mann, George, 120
Martin, Charles, 144
Martin, Harold, 20, 22
Meek, Louis, 106
Memorial Gymnasium, 21, 31, 34, 95, 134, 168
Merris, William, 101, 103
Metropolitan Museum, 98, 112
Miller, Al, 102
Miller, Earle, 31, 74, 75
Miller, Eleanor, 3, 31, 75, 86, 93, 94, 135, 136
Miller, Robert B., 116
Milligan, David, 71
Milligan, Kay, 25
Millikin University, 38
Mills, Richard, 156
Mississippi Valley College Association, 123
Missouri Valley College, 49
Mittlebusher and Tourtelot, 10

Monmouth College, 38
Monroe, James D., 24
Monroe, Karl, 24
Moon rocks, 158, 159
Morgan-Scott Medical Society, 163
Morrell Act, 29, 78
Mundinger, Donald C., 166, 173
Munk, Mary, 50
Munroe, Ogden, 101
Museum of Science, 98

National Defense Student Loan (NDSL), 53, 54
National Endowment for the Humanities, 155, 156, 163
National Science Foundation, 53, 148
Neill, Stephen, 28
Norbury, Garm, 4, 16, 60, 75, 88
North Central Association, 109
North Park College, 123
Northwestern University, 65, 109, 140, 159

O'Brien, Leo "Doc," 117
Ogilvie, Richard (Gov.), 140, 149
Ogishima, Yasuko, 111, 112
Operation Co-Ed, 33
Osage orange, 79
Oxford University, 17
Oxtoby, Robert, 44

Passavant Hospital, 58
Pauls, Rolf, 151, 152
Payap College, 111
Penstone, Bruce, 164
Percy, Charles, 86, 87, 140
Phi Beta Kappa, 5, 19, 27, 31, 94
Pilcher, Fred, 83
Pixley, Ruth Badger, 25, 73, 93, 120
Pixley Hall, 35, 130, 168
Prairie Conference, 120
Presbyterian Church, 2, 16, 20, 29, 30, 31, 37, 38, 41, 69, 77, 80, 84, 111, 114, 115, 122, 136

Index

Presbyterian Life, 23, 41
Princeton University, 13, 21, 35, 80
Principia, 104, 123
Rainbolt, Mary Louise, 94, 120
Rammelkamp, Charles Henry Jr., 80
Rammelkamp, Charles Henry (President), 13, 31, 69, 109
Rammelkamp, Mrs. Charles, 13, 80, 109
Rammelkamp, T. C., 80
Rammelkamp Chapel, 34, 35, 53, 80, 81, 82, 83, 106, 119, 149, 168
Ramsey, Steve, 26
Rantz, Frank, 6
Reader's Digest, 28, 86, 121
Reid, Charlotte Thompson, 85, 117, 147, 173
Reneker, Robert W., 137
Reuter, Palma, 82
Robinson, Carl, 76
Rockefeller Foundation, 5, 68
Rockford College, 38
Roman Catholic, 16, 115, 119
Roosen, William, 76, 85
Roosevelt, Franklin D., 45
Roosevelt University, 21
Routt, 69
Rowland, Tom, 103
Rundquist, Anita, 79
Russell, C. B., 81
Russell House, 33, 105
Ryan, Carole McNamara, 53, 83, 94
Ryan, Charles J., 156
Sangamon State University, 61, 62
School for the Blind, 69
School for the Deaf, 47, 69
Schramm, Leah, 12, 75
Seator, Lynette, 130
Selden, William, 6, 13, 35, 59, 100, 132
Sesquicentennial Fund, 158
Seybold, Ethel, 3, 36, 70, 94, 156, 157
Shepherd, John, 117
Sibert, Robert S., 137
Siefkin, Forest, 71, 76
Silliman University, 2
Simon, Paul, 140
Simpson, Sid, 33
Singh, Vidyapati, 118
Slater Food Service, 50, 143
Smith, Alma, 75
Smith, E. Dwight, 14
Smith, Frances McReynolds, 116, 137
Smith, Joe Patterson, 31, 49, 53, 74, 95, 121
Smith, Mortimer, 31
Smith, Paul, 82
Smith, Ralph, 47, 152
Smith, Rufus, 134
Smith House, 33, 134
Specht, John, 108
Staley, Geraldine, 71
Steers, Donald, 164
Stewart, Malcolm F., 70, 85, 86, 118, 154
Stone, W. Clement, 95, 96
Stratton, William (Gov.), 47
Strawn, Jacob, 108
Struever, Stuart, 159
Student Center, 130, 135, 168
Stuesey, Dwight, 4
Sturtevant, Julian M. (President), 135, 145
Sturtevant, Julian Munson, 145
Sturtevant Hall, 6, 33, 40, 168
Sullivan, William (student), 164
Sullivan, William J. (Trustee), 161
Summers, Ronald, 164
Tanner Library, 8, 31, 35, 83, 106
Tapingkae, Amnuay, 111
Thomas, Benjamin, 6, 45
Thompson, James (Gov.), 143
Thwaite, Walter E., 73, 75
Tong, Ts'ing-Hi, 106, 118, 121

197

Index

Toynbee, Arnold, 57
Truman, Harry, 45
Turck, Charles J., 21
Turner, Jonathan Baldwin, 34, 52, 54, 77, 78, 79, 105
Turner Hall, 34, 106, 117, 121, 168
Turpin, Gary, 101
United Church of Christ, 38, 80, 84, 93, 122
University of Chicago. *See* Chicago, University of
University of Illinois. *See* Illinois, University of
U.S. Steel Foundation, 95
Van Allen, James, 74, 88
VanderWerf, Calvin A., 74, 88
Veith, Judith, 82
Verticchio, Paul C., 156
Viet Nam, 111, 125, 127, 139, 160
Visiting Asian Scholars, 117, 118, 170
Vuylsteke, Richard, 123
Walker, John, 138
Wallace, DeWitt, 28, 121

Walton, Clyde, 79
Walton, William, 119, 137
Washington University, 99, 101
Webber, Elzie, 84, 135
Westminster Fellowship, 23
Whipple Academy, 76
Whipple Hall, 33, 35, 40, 92, 106, 137, 168
Whitney Foundation, 85, 86
Who's Who in America, 25
Wilson, Carol, 88
Wilson, Carroll B., 12, 75
Wilson, Leonard, 23, 24
Wood, Raymond, 46
Woodcock, Lyle S., 120, 121
Woodruff, Donna, 82
Wright, Courtney Crouch, 52

Yale Band, 30
Yale College (University), 21, 46, 77, 112, 145
Yates, Richard, 13
Yeager, Iver F., 49, 85, 110, 118, 122, 153, 154, 164

Zeigler, Elizabeth, 120, 140

/378.773C1357C1/